To Hell I Must Go

Rod Sadler

outskirtspress
DENVER, COLORADO

The opinions expressed in this manuscript are solely the opinions of the author and do not represent the opinions or thoughts of the publisher. The author has represented and warranted full ownership and/or legal right to publish all the materials in this book.

To Hell I Must Go
The True Story of Michigan's Lizzie Borden
All Rights Reserved.
Copyright © 2015 Rod Sadler
v3.0

Cover Photo © 2015 Rod Sadler. All rights reserved - used with permission.

This book may not be reproduced, transmitted, or stored in whole or in part by any means, including graphic, electronic, or mechanical without the express written consent of the publisher except in the case of brief quotations embodied in critical articles and reviews.

Outskirts Press, Inc.
http://www.outskirtspress.com

ISBN: 978-1-4787-5103-8

Outskirts Press and the "OP" logo are trademarks belonging to Outskirts Press, Inc.

PRINTED IN THE UNITED STATES OF AMERICA

For my family

Acknowledgements

There are so many people that I'd like to thank and acknowledge who assisted in my effort to write this book. The first and foremost is my dad, Keith Sadler. He shared the story of my great grandfather and his tenure as the sheriff of Ingham County, which subsequently led to locating the badge, gun, handcuffs and other family treasures kept by our cousin, John MacDonald who, sadly, has passed. Researching more information about my great grandfather led to the discovery of a bizarre murder in Williamston and ultimately this project.

I'd also like to thank Mitch Lutzke. Mitch is a teacher, author, town historian, and friend, and he was instrumental in sharing information about Williamston and some of the history behind the Haney murder. He provided continued suggestions regarding publishing this book and ongoing encouragement.

In addition, the following people all contributed to this book in some way: John MacDonald, Cloyce Odell, R. B. Westbrook, Amy Westbrook, Brad Johnson, Linda Siciliano, Kevin Ingram, George Sinas, Tonya Canfield, and Steve Westlake.

I'd also like to thank the Williamston Depot Museum, the Northeast Ingham Emergency Services Authority, the State of Michigan Library, the Archives of Michigan, the Ingham County Genealogical Society, National Police Gazette Enterprises, LLC, and the Michigan Supreme Court Historical Society.

Finally, I'd to thank my editors, Michael Woodworth and Lisa Wheatcraft, who spent many hours making corrections, suggestions, and words of encouragement to keep this project on track.

Table of Contents

Preface vi

The Sheriff 1

The Murderess 24

The Awful Deed 42

The Inquest 63

The Jail 71

The Circuit Court 88

The Asylum 114

The Final Years 128

Notes 146

Bibliography 149

Endnotes 154

Preface

"*What is Past is Prologue.*" These words are inscribed at the National Archives. Today, for a "young" writer like me, these words couldn't be more true. I use the word "young" for a couple of reasons. I believe that a person is only as young as he or she may feel. Having just passed the mid-century mark myself, I don't believe that's old. My son saw it differently, however, when he reminded me on my 50th birthday that my life was half over. (*Chuckle...pause...wondering.*) More to the point, I use the word "young" because it conveys the sense of a novice or beginner. In terms of this book, I am a new author trying to detail a murder in small-town America that occurred over 100 years ago with somewhat limited information. The past is my beginning. What is Past is Prologue.

Sharing the past...my past when it comes to family history...is something I hadn't planned, nor was sharing the past in the context of a murder. But I realized one day while doing genealogical research that my great grandfather had played a part in vicious events occurring on April 23, 1897, in the same small town where I had played as a child.

Even today a murder, in and of itself, would shake a small community to its very core. The very nature of this murder is so gruesome that, when I mention it, the reply is usually in the form of a question when people ask in disbelief, "Williamston?"

The unique part of this heinous crime centers not only on the murderess, but also my grandfather who was the Ingham County Sheriff when it occurred. Unique to me, but for many years it was a forgotten piece of family history.

The murder had become a forgotten piece of Williamston's history too, much like small towns across America that share interesting stories long since forgotten, stories that only come to light when someone stumbles across a record of the events fortuitously. That happened in this case.

My dad, Keith Sadler, was responsible for sparking my interest only because of my law enforcement connection in the family. It wasn't long after my start in police work when he shared the genealogical tidbit with me: my great, great grandfather had been the sheriff of Ingham County in 1897. More than that, he thought a cousin might still have his badge and gun.

I had already been working for two or three years in law enforcement. I had started my career as a reserve police officer in Williamston. I had grown up there. My dad was born and raised there. For six years I resided in the same house where he was born. I called Williamston my hometown. But I had never given a second thought to the history of Williamston or my great grandfather when I was working there. I was a young man who knew what I wanted to do after high school, and I was doing it. It didn't take long after my stint as a reserve officer when I was hired for my first paying job as a cop in the neighboring community of Webberville.

Every so often, dad would remind me about the family heritage.

Not wanting to spend an entire career working on a small town police force, I moved on to a higher-paying job in law enforcement with Lansing Community College's Police and Public Safety Department. The wage was good, and I had already worked as a student aide there while getting my Associate's Degree in law enforcement. I often wondered what really sparked my interest in my great grandfather's position as the Ingham County Sheriff. I always came back to the same conclusion: police officers at Lansing Community College received their police authority through the Ingham County Sheriff's Office. They were sworn in as Ingham County deputies. As one of them, my badge read "Ingham County Deputy Sheriff." In hindsight I guess there's really no question.

Still, every so often, dad would remind me about great grandpa Rehle. Typically I'd respond, "Oh yeah, that's right," and busy myself with some other task. But I felt a connection too strong to resist.

The stage was set. I asked dad to call our cousin who still had grandpa's badge, gun and handcuffs. I had probably only met my cousin John MacDonald two or three times in my life, but I was really looking forward to this. If he really did have the artifacts, I would take a photo and frame it next to a picture of the badge I wore.

That day was a thrill. We met John at his home in Birmingham, just north of Detroit. While I knew John was a cousin, I still didn't quite know the family connection. It would become much clearer later. John and his wife were the most gracious hosts. He brought out a metal box, which obviously was an old ammunition box, and slowly opened it. There was paper covering the contents. He carefully peeled it back. There, lying on top, was a folded piece of cardboard taped on one side. He pulled the tape away, unfastening the improvised cardboard folder. Behold! A small metal badge inscribed with my great grandfather's name and the words "Ingham County Sheriff." After staring at the badge for a moment, I set it to one side, excited to see what other treasures were within the metal container.

And what treasures there were! The gun...a .38 caliber Hopkins and Allen nickel-plated, break-top revolver. I couldn't believe it. The holster...a leather piece manufactured to slide inside a pant pocket in 1897. The ammunition...two boxes of ammunition. The business card with my great grandfather's name and political affiliation. The extras....a worn leather sap...a hand-carved match box from an inmate at the jail. It was all more than I ever expected.

There were several photos taken that day. I laid my badge next to my great grandfather's and photographed them together. I photographed everything.

I treasured those photos, but for some reason I never framed them.

It was 1987 when I was hired by the Eaton County Sheriff's Office. Shortly after beginning my career with Eaton County, I was contacted by a former captain from Ingham County. Versille Babcock had retired from Ingham County and was now their department historian. He was trying to find as many photos as possible of men who had served as the Ingham County Sheriff through the years. He had heard about my family connections. I shared my photos with him, and he shared some with me. Although I didn't realize it at the time, I was starting to build the foundation for this book.

In my spare time I decided to start digging into my great grandfather's background. The Mason Public Library was a repository of old newspapers from around the time he had served as sheriff. I was paging through those looking for any article that might resemble something about an election or a crime he might have investigated.

AWFUL DEED was the title of an article that caught my attention. The time period was right. It was front page on April 29, 1897. My great grandfather would have been the sheriff. I wondered what this was about. "*Mrs. Haney Murdered by Her Son's Insane Wife*" was the subtitle. This should be an interesting read. "*Old Lady's Head Found on a Plate by the Husband.*" This was getting good. "*It Had Been Chopped Off With a Sharp Ax.*" The article started with the words *Williamston, Mich., April 23, 1897*. In disbelief, I couldn't help but pause and re-read the title of the article and the subtitles. This was the beginning.

Over the next several years, I would occasionally gather a little more information here and there about my family history. One day my dad mentioned that our cousin John was getting older, and he had told my dad that he was thinking about donating my great grandfather's badge, gun, and other things to the Ingham County Sheriff's Office. Dad suggested I write to John and see if he would consider giving them to me in order to keep them in the family. It wasn't long after the letter when dad received a call from John. In a subsequent telephone call to dad he agreed. I couldn't have been more excited.

My interest in writing a book about the murder, and my great grandfather's involvement was growing. With the advent of the Internet, and online digital collections in genealogy, newspapers, photos, and other things, research became so much easier, though there was still a great deal of legwork to be done.

It was after I retired when I really started this project. Having the badge, gun, handcuffs and other things, I was able to locate photos of various people mentioned in the news articles. I started to save those. My search turned to seeking information about the house where the murder occurred, a photo of the murderess, or anything about the murder itself.

Some might consider social media the downfall of our society. Others use it to their advantage. I was in the latter category. I had learned of a local historian in Williamston, Cloyce Odell. Mr. Odell had numerous photos from the late 1800s and early 1900s. I contacted him through the Internet and asked if he knew of the murder and where it had occurred. While he didn't know the address, he knew the name of the family that had lived in the house in the 1940s, and also told me the house no longer existed. I knew from reading the old newspaper articles the house had been very near to the railroad tracks. Unfortunately the articles never mentioned the exact location. After Mr. Odell provided me with the name of the family that had lived there in the forties, I did a quick check on a genealogical website and discovered a draft card of the man who had lived there and listed the address...320 Elevator Street. I paused. I had been in that house! I remembered that house. I knew exactly where that house had stood.

In 1981, after graduating from the police academy, a friend I graduated with had taken me to a small party at that house. His relatives were living there.

It was now 30 years later, and I hadn't seen Russ Westbrook in at least 25 of those years. I called him and Russ confirmed my suspicions: the house by the railroad tracks was 320 Elevator Street.

We arranged a meeting at the site. Russ and his daughter, Amy Stevens, described the house exactly as I remembered it. They knew nothing of its history or the violence that had occurred there in 1897. They told me it had been burned for practice by the Northeast Ingham Emergency Services Authority (formerly the Williamston Fire Department) in the 1990s.

After some digging, NIESA's Assistant Fire Chief Brad Johnson, an old friend, located a photo of the house for me that had been taken a few years prior to the practice burn. Now I was moving.

With small pieces of my project starting to come together, I went to the State Library of Michigan and began looking for additional news articles about the 1897 murder.

I found a number of local Lansing papers but wasn't able to locate any for the time period when the murder occurred. I knew local papers had used segments from a larger article printed in the Detroit Free Press, so I moved on to those microfilms. After finding the original article, I wondered if a follow-up article had been written. I scanned ahead a few days. "*Still in Jail.*" My eyes widened as I stared at a photograph under the headline. It was a young woman. Under the photo it read "*Mrs. Martha Haney.*" I could hardly believe it. I must have stared at that photo for three or four minutes. Copies made….check.

I moved to the Archives of Michigan in the same building. The Archives repository of documents from around the state seemed endless. I had already learned that circuit court records for Ingham County from the late 1800s to the early 1900s were stored there.

I met with a clerk and told her of my quest. She handed me a microfilm roll telling me to search for the person's name and to write down the numbers noted next to the name. Done. They referenced a large notebook with more numbers and directed me to Table 3.

The wooden table seemed huge as I sat there by myself. At another table to my right, a woman sat with a young child looking through archived photos of the city of Lansing. They wore white gloves to protect the prints as they held them. I wondered if I would be provided with white gloves.

A clerk emerged from a back room and rolled a cart up next to my table. On the cart was a box that stored file folders. The clerk removed the top and started to look at the many files contained in the box. He paused, then asked, "People versus Martha Haney?" I could not contain my excitement as I replied, "That's it."

The clerk lifted the file and laid it before me, then walked away. I paused and stared at it then ever-so-slowly opened the file. On top was a smaller folder designed to hold a folded piece of paper. It read *Circuit Court for the County of Ingham, The People of the State of Michigan vs. Martha Haney, April 27, 1897*. On the bottom was a signature, A. M. Cummins, Prosecuting Attorney. I continued. There were 14 pages.

The original court file contained the hand-written complaint and warrant for murder, a written statement from the eyewitness, and a handwritten statement from my great grandfather detailing his involvement. Two other documents piqued my interest. There was another handwritten document describing one of the hearings held by the Justice of the Peace and a typed document from three doctors bearing their original signatures.

"Are you doing okay," I heard someone ask from the front desk. I looked up and said, "I feel like Indiana Jones." There was a chuckle from behind the clerk.

I truly did feel like an archeologist that had just discovered some ancient treasure after having searched for years. As I held those original documents, I ran my fingers across my great grandfather's signature at the bottom of his handwritten statement. Scans made…check.

Subsequent trips to the Archives of Michigan were of significant value. There was more documentation discovered, including records from a private orphanage showing the names of the killer's children, in addition to finding the original blue- prints and maps of the Michigan Asylum for the Dangerous and Criminally Insane.

The Archives of Michigan were full of treasures, but I later discovered the library held even more information in the form of newspaper articles about the murder.

I continued adding sources. It had all become clear now. The names in the news articles all made sense. The sequence of events fell into place. Information gleaned from other sources filled gaps. A timeline could be constructed. There was much more information detailing the gruesome killing that I hadn't had. Everything came together. It was all there…and this is the story.

My goal in this project was to be as accurate as possible in detailing not only the murder itself but the six days that followed. It offers a glimpse of late Nineteenth century law enforcement and criminal court proceedings. In addition, I want the reader to have a clear picture of the people involved and some of the history of mid-Michigan.

Where statements appear in quotations, they have been taken verbatim from a print source such as a newspaper. Recognizing that I cannot reconstruct each person's conduct over a six-day period more than a century ago, I've had to make some assumptions based on my understanding of the law and human nature. The description of the killing comes directly from numerous contemporaneous newspaper accounts from around the mid-Michigan area, in addition to handwritten statements found in the original circuit court file.

[80]

WARRANT FOR Murder

By Virtue of this Warrant, to me directed, I have taken the within named Martha Haney whom I have before John C. Squiers the Justice within named, as I am within commanded.

Dated this 26th day of April 1897

John J. Kohl
Sheriff of Ingham Co.

Courtesy Archives of Michigan

"Serving a human head on a platter is a form of honor little practiced since the time of Herodin's daughter."

-*Kalamazoo Daily Telegraph, April 24, 1897*

THE SHERIFF

As the train engineer applied the brake, the passenger took a pocket watch from his vest and glanced at it. The Wadsworth solid-gold timepiece had been a gift from his wife upon his election. The inscription of a small village on the casing had always reminded him of his homeland. The timepiece read 2:30 p.m.

The shrill of the whistle briefly startled him as it coincided with his quick glance, and it terrified several horses at the Putnam Street crossing. His mind had been somewhere else. The Detroit, Grand Rapids and Western Railroad came to a quick, but gentle stop after passing the intersection. He reached into his coat pocket and pulled out a badge. The engraving read, "J. J. Rehle, Sheriff, Ingham Co, Mich."

Photo by Rod Sadler

The billowing steam from the train's engine hung in the air like a dense fog.

It had been a long and uncomfortable 70-minute ride heading

north from Mason toward Lansing, Michigan's capitol. At Lansing, he switched trains at the Michigan Avenue Depot. His final destination was one of the county's small hamlets located east of the city.

He pinned the badge to his coat as he stepped from one of the train's passenger cars. He didn't wear it every day, but today was different. The telegraphed message had read "Killing in the village. Stop. Come immediately. Stop. Signed J. Loranger."

Steam still continued to pour from the engine's huge smokestack. Sheriff John Jacob Rehle, or "J. J.," as he had come to be known, could hardly see the depot through it. He hesitated for a moment until the steam cleared as several other passengers stepped off the train behind him. In large block letters, the long sign hanging on the west end of the building announced *WILLIAMSTON*.

Incorporated on April 5, 1871, Williamston had become a small business hub within Ingham County over the ensuing decades. It straddled the southeast corner of Williamstown Township and the northern fringe of Wheatfield Township.

Two of the area's first settlers, brothers William and Joseph Putnam, had come from the city of Jackson north to Stockbridge Township, which was located in the southeast corner of Ingham county. Trudging their way to the north and west, they cut a trail that ended at the banks of the Cedar River.

Later this route would come to be known as the Putnam trail, and eventually it became known as Putnam Road. Settling on the banks of the waterway, the two men lived on about 15 acres on the north side of the river. But after harsh weather and poor crop production, the Putnams abandoned their land. In 1839, O. B. and J. J. Williams bought the land.

By 1842 they had built a dam across the river, then a sawmill. A gristmill followed. The millstone they eventually used was brought by wagon from Detroit.

By the time the gristmill had been built, a road had been cut through the area. Mail and passenger lines had been established between Detroit and Lansing. A plank road had been cut through the small village by 1852 and new businesses were beginning to grow. The plank road connecting the state capitol to Detroit required a full day's travel by horse and carriage so the unincorporated village that would later become Williamston seemed an ideal place to stop for a night's rest.

By the late 1870s, in addition to the saw and gristmills, this fledgling community grew to include foundries and machine shops, carriage works, planing mills, marble works, stave manufactures, banks, coal mining operations, a newspaper, and local physicians. Religious orders began to take hold in the community as well, including Lutherans, Baptists, and Catholics.[1] The Catholics were the first to have a place of worship built, naming their new church after Saint Mary. It was located at the corner of High Street and Cedar Street.

Williamston had established itself as a thriving village.

As he glanced around, J. J. thought his deputy might be waiting for him inside the new train depot. His mind recounted recent history and he recalled that this was actually the village's third depot.

The first had been built in 1871 by the Detroit, Lansing and Lake Michigan Railroad. It burned in 1886 when a fire started in the baggage room. A second depot was built by the Detroit, Lansing and Northern Railroad in 1887. At least some of the residents of the growing village weren't happy with the miserly budget for the new building, and they voiced their concerns in the local paper, *The Enterprise*..."Our citizens have neglected a duty to the community in allowing this little $400 concern, which is not as good as the old one, to be erected at an important station as this." Despite these objections the depot was built within the $400 budget. It didn't last long. In 1892 citizen Ed Lawlor discovered the depot was on fire. He quickly notified the station agent, James Kehoe, of the growing inferno. The building was destroyed before Kehoe had a chance to even notify the hook-and-ladder volunteers. The depot was a total loss.[2]

The railroad through Williamston changed several times over the latter part of the 19th Century. Having survived the 1893 depression, it was still making a profit in 1895. In 1896, the DLN Railroad went into receivership, and on January 1, 1897, it became the Detroit, Grand Rapids and Western Railroad. The DGRW Railroad incorporated Grand Rapids, Lansing and Detroit, but also included the Saginaw Valley and St. Louis, Saginaw and Grand Rapids, and the Saginaw and Western. It would eventually become the Pere Marquette Railway in 1899.

Sitting on the north side of the railroad tracks, the newest 21-by-56 foot railroad depot, after having been rebuilt twice over the previous 11 years, was located near Railroad Street and Cedar Street. It opened in January of 1893 and featured a beautiful southern pine interior.[3]

Williamston Railroad Depot, Courtesy Williamston Depot Museum and Cloyce Odell

Directly across from the depot to the south was the back of J. W. Linn's Freight and Grain Elevator where tile, cement, feed, and various other sundries were sold to local farmers and townsfolk.

As passengers began to depart from the train, some began the short walk to the village. Others walked along the wooden passenger platform toward the building. Most, if not all of them, were likely unaware of what had occurred less than three hours earlier. As J. J. paused, a woman bumped into him when she stumbled over a board on the wooden platform that surrounded the depot and extended to the west toward Putnam Street. In true gentleman fashion, he turned and said, "Pardon me, Madame," as if it were somehow his fault. She noticed an accent as she glanced at the badge pinned to his lapel. She nodded and continued toward the building.

Ingham County Sheriff John Jacob Rehle

Apprehension set in as J. J. made his way toward the passenger station. He had no idea what to expect. He didn't see the deputy standing outside so he moved toward the door. The sound of his boots on the wooden walkway seemed to echo as he made his way inside. He walked through the door on the west end of the building.

The ticket office was just inside, it's open window framed in wood with a heavy metal grate across the opening. J. J. nodded to the station agent seated in a wooden chair behind a cluttered desk. The agent glanced up as he heard the door open and recognized J. J. Even during the day, the agent's office seemed dim, and the soft glow of the light hanging over his desk created a shadow against the wall. The top of the desk was littered with papers, but a raised shelf behind the agent held neatly stacked books. Having fully expected the arrival of the law, he nodded at the sheriff.

J. J. turned to his right and walked through another door into the main baggage area. In the far corner, standing next to the Duke Cannon heating stove used to warm the small building, stood Deputy J. W. Loranger.

The Loranger name was well known in and around the Williamston area. All of the Lorangers were musicians, and until the passing of their patriarch, Eli, the Loranger family provided music for the majority of the dances and entertainment around town.

Loranger turned as he heard J. J. enter the room. The two lawmen moved toward each other as Loranger extended an afternoon greeting. The smell of the deputy's cigar smoke permeated the small building. The sheriff nodded, still wary of the unfolding events. Not wanting his apprehension to show, he took a deep breath. With his slight German accent, he acknowledged Loranger's greeting with a simple hello.

At over six feet tall, Sheriff Rehle's thick mustache accented his well-groomed appearance. A small goatee was the perfect complement to his broad face, and, at the age of 50, his thick black hair showed no signs of graying. With his wool coat buttoned, the black silk tie he wore laid neatly in a proper knot over his white shirt and vest. He had pinned the badge, more a ceremonial gift than anything official, over his left coat pocket.

Known for his honesty and fairness over the years, he was no stranger to local township government, but today was much different from his experiences as a former township official. Today he was the elected Ingham County Sheriff.

Well-liked among his constituents, J. J. won his bid for sheriff in the November 3, 1896, general election, and he carried himself with pride. Two months after the election he moved his wife from their rural Wheatfield Township farm to the city of Mason, the heart of Ingham County, to begin his two-year term. For now the Rehle's new home would be a residence attached to the jail.

Born in Bavaria, Germany in September 1846, Johann Jacob Rehle, Jr., came to America with his parents, Johann Sr. and Christine. Johann Sr., a librarian, had served faithfully in the German army. After only four years of marriage following his discharge, he decided to move his family to America seeking a better life. Boarding a steamship called *The Louvre*, they arrived in the United States in 1850. With J. J. just three years old, his parents wasted no time settling on a farm in Greenfield Township in Wayne County near Detroit. After a sojourn of five years, the Rehle family moved to Ingham County in the heart of Michigan, settling in the northern part of Wheatfield Township with several other families of German ancestry. These families included the Linns, Stoffers, Lotts, Zimmers, Rohbochers, and Karns.

J. J.'s father built the family homestead on Noble Road a few miles southwest of the unincorporated Village of Williamston where he farmed his 80 acres and began a new life for his small family. He was quiet, industrious and a law-abiding citizen of the township. His geniality was one of his strongest traits and he slowly took his wife and child from a life of poverty to comfortable living. Being of strong Lutheran faith, Johann Sr. raised J. J. in the German traditions brought from their homeland, teaching him the strength and integrity of being an honest man.

As J. J. grew older, he farmed the family land with his father until 1869 when he started on his own. By that time they had acquired 300 acres in Wheatfield Township. Originally purchased from a man named Sloan, the Rehle land had large deposits of sand and gravel that formed beautiful hills along the creek running through the property. It was said that their land had some of the best improvements in the township.[4]

J. J. met and fell in love with a woman also of German descent named Sarah Landenberger. Sarah lived in Watertown Township near Grand Ledge in neighboring Clinton County.

Despite her slight build, Sarah was a strong woman. Born in 1847 in Liverpool, Ohio, she had moved to mid-Michigan with her family at the age of five. A few inches shorter and a year younger than J. J., together they were a perfect couple, and in June of 1869, they were married.

Sarah kept her hair short and worked diligently alongside her husband. This was a hard life, but it was not without reward. In their first year together as husband and wife, Sarah and J. J. welcomed their first child, Charles. Three years later, their daughter Anna was born. In 1879, Anna's sister Elizabeth followed, and in 1886, J. J.'s family was complete when Sarah gave birth to Etta.

J. J. and Sarah's two-story farmhouse on Burkley Road in Wheatfield Township sat across a field to the southeast from his father Johann's. A mere quarter mile separated them. With their combined acreage, Johann and J. J. worked the land together.

Beginning in 1871, politics became a way of life for J. J. That year he was elected Wheatfield Township treasurer. He was re-elected the next year, and he was once again elected in 1876. He held the Township Treasurer position for the ensuing six years and would have continued in that office except for his father's failing health. By 1882, Johann needed constant care.

J. J. raised his son Charles just as Johann had raised him. To the Rehles, politics wasn't a thirst for power but an opportunity to take on responsibilities and serve the community they lived in. Besides his other political positions through the 1880s, J. J. also served as president of the Farmer's Alliance in Ingham County.[5]

J. J.'s desire to serve as the county sheriff started more in jest among his friends. At a township meeting one night, after hearing J. J. speak, a local farmer simply suggested that he ought to take on the task of sheriff. J. J. chuckled, brushing off the idea. But in the back of his mind, he began to wonder. After all, he had been designated township constable in 1880.[6]

One evening, after dinner, he waited for the most favorable time and brought up the idea to Sarah. She hesitated, thinking for a long moment. Sarah knew her husband had a strong and honest reputation, and she knew he would be a sound sheriff. J. J. was sitting in the parlor with her. She got up from her chair and walked behind him. Placing her arms around her husband, she urged him to do it. A spark had ignited the flame, and J. J. first ran for sheriff in 1890 on the populist ticket leading his party. J. J. was defeated in the election that year, but that setback in no way diminished his desire for the office of sheriff.

The 1896 election was seen as a new era in politics. Key elements in past Presidential elections had been largely based on whether the country should be governed by rural farmers' urban-based industrial interests. America's monetary policy was coming to a head in this election because of the economic depression in 1893. President Grover Cleveland had split the Democratic Party in his second term over his fiscal policy. There were a few democrats who agreed with the President's support of the gold standard, but other rural populist democrats believed that inflation was the key to raising prices and easing the debt on American farmers. Their idea was centered on "free silver," or the unlimited coinage of silver at a ratio of 16 to 1 against the gold coin.[7]

J. J., still a populist democrat, was an advocate of what came to be known as the "free silver" movement. Proud of his party affiliation, he made sure it was printed on his campaign business cards. As the 1896 elections neared, the local newspapers were inundated with endorsements for both republicans and democrats.

At the same time J. J. was running for the office of county sheriff, a Nebraska democrat was in the thick of the race for the U. S. Presidency. Lawyer William Jennings Bryan gave a speech in Chicago at the Democratic National Convention that would later be characterized as the finest oration in American history. His position, supported by J. J., was reflected in a speech recorded by the *Ingham County Democrat*. In that speech William Jennings Bryan said, "You shall not press down upon the brow of labor this crown of thorns; you shall not crucify mankind upon a cross of gold!" Bryan, attacking McKinley's adherence to the gold standard, won the democratic nomination.

J. J. Rehle's Business Card, Photo by Rod Sadler

The excitement of the upcoming election was building to a crescendo. In October, the democratic candidate for the presidency made a tour through Michigan. William Jennings Bryan was scheduled to pass through Ingham County and make a five-minute stop in Leslie, a five-minute stop in Mason, and then head to the capitol city, Lansing, where he was expected to speak for about three-and-a-half hours.

Just before Bryan's tour through the Great Lakes State, the following was reported in a local paper about just one township in Ingham County:

> "Leroy Township has been canvassed by one who knows nearly everyone politically and found about 420 free silverites [sic] and about 30 gold bugs."[8]

With Bryan coming through Ingham County, local merchants took advantage of the event by incorporating his name in their advertising. For example, Webb and Whitman, a clothier in Mason, touted a "Bryan in Mason" overcoat sale. This would surely be an election to remember.

Just a week before the election, instructions were printed clearly outlining how the citizen democrats of Ingham County were expected to vote:

> "Your ticket is the third on the ballot in this county, your vignette is a silver dollar containing a picture of William Jennings Bryan, your gallant leader."[9]

On November 3, 1896 the republican presidential candidate William McKinley was elected President of the United States. William Jennings Bryan was defeated. But while a republican was elected as the President of the United States, Ingham County elected the populist democrat, John J. Rehle, as it's new sheriff. J. J. defeated his closest opponent, Marshall Campbell, by only 560 votes. He defeated a third candidate, Frank Maher, by an astounding 5626.

J. J. took office at the start of the 1897 New Year. It was on January 7 when the $10,000 bond he was required to file as the newly elected chief law enforcement officer of the county was approved by the Board of Supervisors. The bond was filed by Judson Salisbury. Joe Banly of Wheatfield Township, and C. D. Colby and B. F. Potts were listed as sureties. At that time, the board allowed the city marshal of Lansing 30 cents per day to house prisoners. The same amount was authorized for the sheriff to house convicts at the jail. The board refused to tolerate any extravagance. The previous sheriff had submitted a bill for $1435.40, which equaled 40 cents per day for housing. He was only allowed $1120.05.

J. J. knew he would need an undersheriff, and in his first month he appointed his son-in-law Martin to the position. Martin had married J. J. and Sarah's daughter, Anna, in 1892. George Landenburger was appointed as a turnkey, and William Whitehead, Herbert Ripley, and J. W. Loranger were designated as deputies.[10] Both Whitehead and Loranger were from the Webberville area, a short five miles or so east of Williamston. J. J. needed deputies in several of the small hamlets around the county. In addition to Whitehead, Loranger and Ripley, he appointed William Harder to serve as an Ingham County deputy in the small village of Onondaga. He chose G. D. Campbell as the physician who would attend to any female prisoners at the Ingham County Jail.

As her husband settled into his new role as county sheriff, J. J.'s wife Sarah discovered their new life was much different than the quiet farming life she had become used to. Now she was exposed to the misdeeds of others. Yet Sarah was known to always have a good word for those who had erred.

Sarah enjoyed the brief limelight of foiling a jail break later that year, but J. J.'s new job as the sheriff was mostly mundane and included a host of commonplace duties. The routine of sending out notices to the township and city clerks about the general spring election following a county vote struck J. J. as a little ironic. After all, he had once been a township supervisor and had received the same reports from other sheriffs in years past.

At times J. J. may have felt wedded to his position as sheriff, but there was no honeymoon period after he took office. In early January Thomas Cook was convicted of Enticing a Sixteen-year-old for Concubinage. It was J. J.'s duty to make sure Cook made it to the state prison in Jackson safely.[11] Around that same time Florence Bailey was convicted of Lewd and Lascivious Cohabitation and sentenced to the Detroit House of Corrections.[12] Yet again, J. J. made sure she arrived without incident. And he was also called upon to make a trip to Denver, Colorado where he took custody of a prisoner and brought him back to Michigan.

J. J. soon discovered that, while much of his work was related to law enforcement, there were times when community relations took center stage. He didn't mind a bit.

A man named James Edwards was arrested for public drunkenness and incarcerated at the jail. While Edwards was spending his time behind bars, a woman tried to enlist J. J. to persuade the inmate to marry her. She told J. J. that she had "a half acre of golden vegetables at home and felt compelled to manage the matter of making Edwards happy." J. J. felt sorry for the love-struck woman, but he wasn't a matchmaker. The sheriff declined, smiling to himself as he turned to more pressing matters.

It was a busy time as J. J. began to settle in as sheriff. There were needed repairs to the jail and the courthouse, including painting and repairing furniture. He and County Chairman Seely were appointed as a committee of two authorized to make the needed repairs to county offices.

At the same time, the city of Lansing, which already served as the seat of state government, was pushing to be named as the county seat. A board on which J. J. was a member visited the city for 5 ½ days. For his attendance and research into the possibility of naming Lansing as the county seat, rather than Mason, he received $11.00 reimbursement.[13] The city's efforts proved unsuccessful. Mason remained the official county seat.

In late January, J. J. and Sarah left Mason and headed to Grand Ledge, a small city in neighboring Eaton County to visit Sarah's brother Jacob Landenburger. The local paper caught wind of his visit and stopped by during the Rehles' visit. J. J. did not hesitate to report that business was booming at the Ingham County Jail.

In February, Probate Judge Porter, Court Agent James Welhings, and County Supervisors H. C. Freeland, W. L. Reed, and George Dunckel inspected the jail and concluded that J. J. was managing it quite well. Their report indicated there were 31 prisoners at the time of the inspection and all of the bedding appeared to be in good condition. The inspectors recommended a good flush-water closet be installed on the second floor for the Rehles' use.

Day-to-day law enforcement in Ingham County went on. On March 8, J. J. arrested Leroy Emmons for deserting his wife. Mrs. Emmons had made a complaint against her husband for deserting her and their six-week-old child. On March 10, Emmons was found guilty and fined $6.35 in court costs. After paying his fine, he returned to his wife and child.

March started much like the first two months of 1897 with J. J. transporting prisoners to various locations. William Babcock, convicted of being a common "tippler", was taken to the Detroit House of Corrections to serve out his sentence.

Cooperation between the Sheriff's Office and the Lansing police was not uncommon. Lansing's Police Chief Sanford worked closely with J. J. On March 17, J. J. and Deputy Ferris, along with three Lansing police officers, raided a house of ill repute. Seven females were arrested. Fourteen males met the same fate.

The influx of prisoners at the jail varied from day to day depending on the workload of other lawmen in the county. On April 18, the Lansing Police Department brought a batch of hobos to the county jail, filling it over its limited capacity. The delivery of several hobos at one time became a regular strain on available resources.

On one trip to the Detroit House of Corrections in Janurary, instead of delivering prisoners, J. J. returned to Ingham County with three witnesses who had been confined in Detroit. They would testify against Robert Martin, who had been charged with furnishing spirituous liquors to prisoners in the county jail. Martin was found guilty and allowed 20 days to appeal for a new trial. He posted his $500 bond and was released. It seemed that J. J.'s entire first several months in office were filled with daily travel.

On March 3, Circuit Judge Rollin Person granted Martin a new trial.[14] Little did Judge Person know that he and Sheriff Rehle would meet again the following month, but that meeting wouldn't involve something as trifling as a charge of supplying whiskey to jail inmates. Rather, it would involve a hideous crime of a much grander scale.

The everyday tasks of a county sheriff seemed to fit J. J. very well. He enjoyed his new job and enjoyed working with the people who elected him as their sheriff. But nothing in his first four months as the county's top lawman, or anything in his remaining 20 months would compare with what he was about to bear witness to on April 23, 1897. The events of that day would compel him to appear before Judge Person again.

J. W. Loranger was the only deputy in the village of Williamston that day. Inside the depot, J. J. greeted him with an outstretched hand. The warmth from the coal stove in the corner helped to dismiss the early spring chill. J. J. and his deputy stepped out of the depot and into a dull, cloudy and cool April day. Rain, sometimes hard, had fallen continuously. It didn't take long for the dirt streets to quickly turn into mud.

J. J. first glanced to the west. When he turned back toward the east he still couldn't see his objective. The house was just beyond view. The stave mill, in addition to the Freight Elevator, sat between J. J. and his destination. Loranger had already told him where it had occurred.

The two lawmen crossed the tracks on foot and passed by the west end of J. W. Linn's Freight Elevator. They walked in silence. Passing between the building and the rows of neatly- stacked clay tiles waiting to be sold, Rehle and Loranger rounded the corner of the building and headed east along the muddy street, their strides unintentionally in unison. To the right stood a large, three-story building with a shingled canopy stretching across the entire front of the building. Painted in large letters across the upper two-thirds of the wooden structure were the words COLD STORAGE. Under that appeared the name F. P. VanBuren. With their pace slowed by the soft pull of mud on their boots, J. J. thought for just a moment how surreal everything seemed.

Passing the front of the cold storage building, the sheriff and his deputy continued their journey toward the small house. It was only a short distance now, perhaps 500 feet. As they passed the drying kilns for the stave mill, and then the mill itself, many eyes were upon them. Nearby workers slowed their operations as the two men slowly went by.

There sat the domicile, if one chose to call it that. In front of the structure a small crowd of people milled about. Some were friends. Others were curiosity seekers. A few of the women were softly crying, gently wiping their tears with kerchiefs. Some children stood among them. Horses attached to carriages cluttered the intersection. No one had dared enter the house, and no one spoke a word as the two officers approached. A hush settled on the scene like a low-hanging winter cloud. Loranger had men posted outside to keep gawkers away. Everyone knew the Sheriff was on his way.

J. J. could feel the crowd's frozen stare. Loranger had already told him what had happened, and although he knew no one was left inside, he still felt uneasy. He reached into his front-right pant pocket out of habit more than anything else. He felt the weight of the nickel plated Hopkins and Allen .38 revolver. It was right where he always carried it, contained in a small leather holster. Five extra bullets were attached to the outside of the holster. In his left coat pocket he carried a heavy pair of shackles. A hundred things were racing through J. J.'s mind, and for just a split second he questioned why he had ever wanted to be the sheriff. He certainly had never expected anything like this.

They paused. After hearing Loranger describe the hideous scene, J. J. still found it hard to believe the reported brutality of the attack. He turned toward his deputy. He asked who had custody of the perpetrator. Loranger replied that he had sent for the other village deputy, Bill Whitehead, as soon as he had heard of the killing. He reported Whitehead was down at the village lockup with the prisoner waiting for them.

As they continued toward the house, J. J. eased his grip on the .38 and took his hand out of his pocket. No one noticed. The crowd of onlookers, many of whom knew both Loranger and J. J., slowly backed away. Both men paused again, this time at the front of the house. The curious crowd remained eerily silent as they watched the lawmen's every move.

The residence was a simple building. It had no porch. Only two windows adorned the front of the house, and there was an entrance on the east corner. The front door hung on the remnants of a single hinge. The other hinge had been broken. Sitting on a stone foundation, the house faced to the south toward the railroad tracks that ran a mere 100 feet or so from the front door. J. J. noticed a small window in the foundation on the west side of the house. He could tell there was a cellar. There were no trees around the wooden-framed shack. There was no paint on the house. Weathered boards served as siding. Peering in from the outside, J. J. could see nothing but squalor. Stepping closer, he observed large gouges and holes cut into the wooden door as if someone had hacked away at it.

The Haney House, Circa 1990s, Courtesy Northeast Ingham Emergency Services Authority and Brad Johnson

They moved even closer and Loranger advised J. J. to watch his step. J. J. hesitated as he looked around from the threshold. A large pool of blood lay just beyond the door. It had congealed to a tacky, dark red mass. Large clumps of gray hair were mixed with the blood.[15] Like the gouges in the front door, he could see similar deep cuts into the wooden floor. He slowly went inside, careful to avoid stepping in the carnage. As he crossed into the house, he noticed what was left of a carpet. It had been ripped from the floor, but remnants were still lying about. A chair lay overturned near a corner of the room. Near the chair, a picture frame surrounding broken glass lay on the floor. J. J. noticed there was no picture in the frame. Odd, he thought. Along one wall sat a small sofa covered in blood. A trail of blood led from the front door toward the rear of the house. Clearly the killer's quarry had been dragged across the floor. The blood was smeared; soaked into the wood and what was left of the carpet. J. J. had seen much in his life, but never so much blood.

Facing to the south inside the living room, he noticed a bedroom to his right. There was no door, only a drapery pulled to the side. At a glance, nothing appeared disturbed, at least from where he stood. He followed the smeared blood from the living room into the kitchen, still carefully placing his every step. Loranger was right behind him. As the sheriff slowly entered the next room, without even thinking, his right hand again went instinctively to his pocket. He knew there was no one in the house, but that knowledge did nothing to stop his hand from automatically returning to the concealed gun in his pocket.

J. J. stopped. He was stunned by what lay before him. He had listened to Loranger's description of the home, but this was beyond anything for which he was prepared.

The kitchen sat directly beyond the living room. The trail of blood continued toward the back door located in the kitchen. It left no doubt. A body had been dragged through the house.[16] Now the corpse was on the floor directly in front of him. It was covered with burned clothing. The charred material made the body underneath almost unrecognizable. Only remains of what had once been human hands protruded from the pile. At the opposite end two partially melted women's slippers covered remnants of human feet. The clothing had been soaked in kerosene and set ablaze.[17] The wooden floor was damp around the body from where water had been poured onto it in an effort to douse the flames. Between the legs of the body was a pan of ashes and charred wood that had also been soaked with water. Thus far, J. J. had intentionally kept himself from glancing to his left, but after seeing the body, he knew he had no choice. Loranger had described the scene to him in vivid detail.

His gaze moved ever so slowly upward from the floor. On the table sat filthy dishes encrusted with dried food. More blood….a lot more blood…copious amounts of blood. His survey of the horrific scene stopped. His gaze was frozen on the table's centerpiece. His stomach began to churn. He could hear himself breathing harder now. Disbelief set in.

Saturated in blood with lifeless eyes staring into blank space, an old woman's head sat on a dinner plate in the center of the kitchen table. It was turned toward one particular place setting at the table. Dried blood caked her hair, the plate and the tabletop. There were cuts and bruises about her face. Adding insult to injury, a knife and fork adorned each side of the plate on which her head had been placed.

J. J. was aghast. The sight of the decapitated, charred body of the old woman, her head carefully presented on a dinner plate as if it were the next course to be served, now mixed with the bouquet of seared human flesh, only added to his sudden intestinal misery.

The gruesome scene was almost too much to bear. As he slowly looked around, he refocused on the deplorable conditions and wondered how someone could be so vicious in the killing of an old woman. As he continued his inspection of the home, he entered the bedroom noticed earlier. The window on the west side was broken inward. Broken glass was strewn about the floor and a bed linen had been partially dragged through the broken window.[18] There were small amounts of blood on the windowsill and on the ground outside. The floor was soaked with water, much like the kitchen floor.

Queasiness overtook J. J. again. He started to wretch. He

needed to get outside. He walked quickly toward the back door looking for some escape from the horror. Loranger was right behind him. He stepped over the dark red trail that led toward the heap of human remains. Suddenly, the odor of kerosene mixed with seared human flesh began to overpower him. He started to gag as he raced to the door.

Once outside, the sheriff paused, breathing in the fragrance of wood and sawdust coming from the stave mill next to the house. J. J. had never smelled anything sweeter. Loranger, standing behind him, heard him utter in his soft German accent, "Mein Gott." Loranger didn't speak German, but he understood exactly what his boss had said.

After several seconds of standing and staring at nothing in particular, J. J. turned and looked Loranger straight in the eyes. There was simply nothing that could be said. As the two began their survey of the exterior, droplets of blood on the ground leading from the house out the back door caught their attention. The trail of blood led to some stairs at the rear door. Boards were found lying under the stoop of the ramshackle building. Moving the boards, J. J. saw it: the instrument of death - a blood soaked axe.[19] The manner in which the victim was killed had now become clear. This was the implement used to chop off the old woman's head. The blood seemed to have barely dried. It had slowly dripped off the blade and soaked a small area of the ground underneath. The handle of the axe was covered in coagulated gore. J. J. pulled the axe from its hiding place and handed it to his deputy. Loranger took it, and the men continued their search outside. After rounding the entire exterior of the building and finding nothing more of value, they were satisfied as to the cause and manner of her death.[20]

As they walked back to the front yard, there were gasps from several women. A partially muffled scream broke the somber silence as women in the crowd saw what Loranger carried in his hands. Several horses tied in front of the house stirred. Perhaps it was from the scream. Perhaps it was from the smell of blood that now seemed to permeate everything.

As the two men paused in front of the house, J. J. recognized Fred Rockwell, the village undertaker. Rockwell had moved to Williamston in 1870 after a man named Michael Bowerman had taken him on to work. Bowerman considered Rockwell a master mechanic who could fix anything. Together, they set up a sawmill in LeRoy Township and eventually moved the mill to Rockwell's Wheatfield Township home. Sometime after the move, the mill was destroyed by a fire. Rockwell didn't rebuild the mill, and his business partner took up selling land in the Williamston area. Rockwell turned his attention to the furniture business under the name of Rockwell and Tuttle.[21] He also served as the undertaker. As J. J. and Loranger had been going through the house, Rockwell had heard the news about the killing. He knew he would be needed. Rockwell stopped his horse-drawn hearse in front of the stave mill trying to avoid the crowd. When the sheriff was done with whatever he had to do, Rockwell was certain he would be called upon to take possession of the body.[22] In his funeral car sat a wooden coffin. J. J. and Loranger approached him. While Loranger described the scene to Fred Rockwell, J. J. joined in to caution the undertaker that the victim was an awful sight. Beyond that, J. J. didn't detail the condition of her body. Fred simply nodded. Like J. J. earlier in the day, he didn't really know what to expect, even though word of the killing had spread through the small village like wildfire. J. J. told Rockwell that several of the men posted outside the house to keep people from entering would be more than willing to help him load the body. Rockwell nodded in appreciation.

When J. J. asked Loranger where the killer's husband was, he told J. J. the man was with some friends.

J. J. knew he needed to get to the lockup. Bill Whitehead, the other deputy that Loranger had summoned, was there guarding the prisoner. The sheriff asked Loranger where he had left his horse and carriage and Loranger pointed back toward the depot. J. J. and Loranger started walking in that direction. Fred Rockwell steered his team of horses toward the scene of the killing. Soon he and others standing guard at the crime scene would begin the grim task of gathering up the old woman's remains.

The cold rain began to fall again.

Deputy Loranger, Courtesy Linda Siciliano

THE MURDERESS

Riding in Loranger's carriage, the sheriff and deputy headed north on Putnam Street. Putnam divided the east and west sides of the village, traveling through the center of the small hamlet.

While J. J. had ridden through muddy streets many times, the mud seemed even thicker today slowing their travel seemingly to a crawl. Perhaps that was because the lawmen were in such a hurry to reach the lockup. They passed wooden storefronts and brick buildings with canvas awnings suspended in the April rain on both sides of the street.

J. J. had always loved Williamston. Its streets were lined with large maple trees that cast long shadows across the dirt streets in the summer sun and offered brilliant orange and yellow colors in the fall, making it appear as if the huge trees were afire.

To first-time visitors of the bustling village, it appeared as though the streets were a network of mud flats snaking out of the Cedar River. They were always muddy in wet weather, and, when it was dry, they were incredibly dusty.

J. J. and Loranger rode a few blocks north from the railroad tracks approaching the downtown. Passing the beautiful stone Methodist Church with its tall, stained glass windows at the corner of Middle and Putnam, J. J. noted Beeman's store across the street offering hats and shoes to its longstanding and loyal customers. He knew his wife Sarah was one of those customers.

Across the street was the Austin & Laberteaux Meat Market. J.J. caught the smell of smoked meats emanating from inside as they passed. On the same side of the street a few doors down the townsfolk did their banking at the State Bank. One of the town druggists, F. P. McCarrick, ran his pharmacy across from the bank. Next to McCarrick's was the Liverance Grocery, offering all sorts of goods to the village residents.

Horses attached to carriages were parked alongside the street. Townsfolk wandered about minding to their business, trying to avoid the afternoon showers, until they noticed J. J. and Loranger. All eyes were upon them as they made their way toward city hall. When they reached the Plank Road at the main four corners of the village, Loranger turned his horse toward the east.

Downtown Williamston, Michigan looking west, Courtesy Williamston Depot Museum and Cloyce Odell

A gentle curve in the Plank Road intersected with Putnam Street and divided the town from north to south and east to west. Two blocks to the north, the Cedar River rolled gently through town winding its way toward the dam next to the mill. A small steel bridge spanned the river to allow ingress and egress to northern crossroads.

J. J. glanced at the Andrew's Hotel on the southwest corner. Its small awnings extended from each window of the three-story building. Then he turned his gaze toward the stately National Block Building across from the hotel with its grandiose architecture. On the southwest corner of the main intersection was the town's wooden post office building, while on the southeast corner sat Leisa's Drugstore, completely built with bricks and well known for its curved facade forming the corner of the building that lined both South Putnam and the Plank Road. The town's bandstand was located just west of the main four corners in the middle of the street.

Southeast Corner of Putnam and Grand River, Courtesy Williamston Depot Museum and Cloyce Odell

Now heading east, J. J. could see Meader's Photo Studio on the north side of the street. He and Sarah had had some photos taken there. Several other small shops and stores lined the street. Metal railings separated the sidewalks from the dirt street waiting to secure horses while their owners went about their business in the village.

Williamston was always an idyllic place to J. J.; that is, it had always been an idyllic place…before today.

A block away, on the north side of the street the town hall waited. This two-story brick building was located next to the Opera House and featured a small bell tower in the center. The offices it contained were on the east end. Designed and constructed in 1890 by Hiram Higbee, the building owed its existence mostly to the Federal Voting

Rights Act of 1890 which required a private place for citizens to cast votes in elections. A small park designed to serve community functions and a large statue honoring Eli P. Alexander, a local civil war veteran, sat in front of the building.

Williamston Village Hall, circa 1900, Courtesy Williamston Depot Museum and Cloyce Odell

On the west end of the town hall was a garage. Parked inside was a Clapp and Jones steam fire engine and a large water hose reel used by the hook and ladder volunteers. A two-cell calaboose also sat inside against the back wall of the garage behind the fire equipment. The iron cells, manufactured by E. T. Barnum Iron and Wire Works in Detroit, were heavy square cages. They had been purchased by the village in 1890 at a cost of $225.00. Each cell contained a swinging bunk offering little comfort to those unfortunate enough to be incarcerated.[23]

As he stepped from the buggy, J. J. saw Deputy Whitehead coming toward them from the lockup. He'd been anxiously waiting their arrival. As the clearly nervous Whitehead neared, he shook his head and remarked that the newly jailed murder suspect was certainly an odd one. J. J. was curious and asked Whitehead if the woman had said anything. Whitehead reported the only thing she had said was she had killed her mother-in-law. That was nothing new. She had said the same thing when Loranger arrested her.[24]

Martha Haney, The Detroit Free Press, April 26, 1897

Since leaving the scene of the crime, J. J. had regained his steady character. He told Loranger to go get Dr. Shumway. J. J. knew Doc Shumway personally. He wanted the doctor to examine the prisoner and see if she was as deranged, as both Loranger and Whitehead thought she was. In the meantime, J. J. decided he would try to talk to her.

The village calaboose typically held the occasional disorderly drunkard for a night or two. If there was a hobo passing through with no means of support, he'd likely spend a night in the lockup, be given a sandwich in the morning, and told to move on. But with word of the vicious murder spreading at lightning speed, everyone in the village knew the lockup now held the most notorious guest Williamston's small jail had ever seen.

J. J. entered through the garage door and passed the steam fire engine as he walked toward the back of the room. Despite the fact that he was now out of the cool, spring air, it somehow seemed even colder inside.

The prisoner sat on the floor wrapped in a blanket. Small in stature, she appeared to be about 25 years old, and she had a consumptive look about her.[25] With her hair pulled back, her close-set eyes looked as dark as a cast iron frying pan. J. J. hesitated, then nodded and introduced himself as the sheriff. Silence. The woman stared at the floor. J. J. paused for a long moment. Again, he asked her name. Again, there was nothing but silence.

J. J. stared at the woman, wondering how someone so slight could have acted out so viciously. She was emaciated, almost to point of starvation.[26] The silence was broken by the sound of voices outside the building. J. J. turned and walked back out the garage door. He saw Loranger with Dr. Shumway and Dr. Shaw walking toward the building.

Dr. Frank Shumway was a local physician. A tall, thin man, he wore long sideburns that sharply contrasted with his thinning hair.

The doctor's eyes were deep set eyes and a thick handlebar mustache rested above his thin lips. He was an impeccable dresser. Today Dr. Shumway wore a Cassimere suit and Danbury hat.

Serving as the Village Health Officer in addition to being a general practitioner, the doctor maintained an office that sat east of the village's main intersection not far from the town hall. Well respected within the medical community, Shumway had graduated from Western Reserve College in Cleveland and the Medical Department of Wooster University in 1881. He chose Western Reserve University because his father had received his medical education there. Frank never had the chance to discuss the decision with him however. Frank's father died not long after the boy's third birthday.[27]

Dr. Frank Shumway

When Loranger first appeared at his office, Dr. Shumway asked who had been killed and who the killer was. When Loranger told him the killer was Martha Haney, he recognized her name. Tight-lipped, he slowly nodded. Having seen the woman about town, he had often questioned her lucidity. In fact he was supposed to have seen her that very morning, but she hadn't appeared for her appointment. He would surely come and examine her, but he wanted a second doctor to attend as well, especially if the woman's comprehension was in question. He asked Loranger to get Dr. Shaw, another town physician, and see if he would come along.

J. J. thanked both doctors for coming. He described the horrid murder of the old woman and asked if they might try to examine Martha's mental state. He explained that she wouldn't say anything to him, or anyone else for that matter, other than she had killed her mother-in-law. The doctors agreed to provide whatever assistance they could.

Before going into the lockup, Dr. Shumway told J. J. that Alfred Haney had asked him to speak with his wife that morning because he thought she might be experiencing some problems. The Haneys never showed up at his office.

The physicians quietly entered the lockup. Doc Shumway removed his hat and graciously nodded to the woman seated on the floor inside the cell. Martha glanced toward them, recognizing Dr. Shumway, then turned her gaze back to the floor. She was a pitiful sight. Shumway introduced both himself and Dr. Shaw. There was no response. Doc Shumway tried a second time, asking Martha Haney if she knew where she was. She responded to the question with a slow nod. Shumway glanced at Shaw, then back at Martha. At least the woman had acknowledged their presence. Doc Shumway saw her eyes dart toward them, then away. Doctor Shaw reminded Martha that they were doctors and not lawmen. There was another quick glance from Martha. Shumway continued and told her they had learned something terrible had occurred at her home today. Martha slowly nodded. The doctor asked if Martha could tell them what had happened. In a barely audible voice, Martha said, "I killed my mother-in-law."

Martha slowly raised her head and stared at both men now. But her gaze held nothing; it cut through the men like a sharp knife.

While Doc Shumway and his colleague were examining Martha Haney, J. J. directed Loranger to find Justice McEnally. J. J. knew they would need to conduct an inquest as soon as possible, especially given Martha's mental state.

After Loranger's departure, J. J. and Whitehead leaned against the large red wheels on the steam fire engine and listened intently just inside the garage door. Doc Shumway, whom Martha seemed to recognize the most asked, "Can you tell us what happened at your home?" There was another long pause. Just as the two doctors were about to give up and turn toward the door, Martha said she'd had a quarrel with her mother-in-law and that the old woman had struck her. The two men stopped and turned back toward the cell. She told them she put a picture of her kids in a frame, but the frame belonged to Alfy's mother and they got into a fight over it.[28] She continued, "She had me down, and I made my mind up I would kill her." Shumway and Shaw glanced at one another. Doc Shumway turned toward J. J. and Deputy Whitehead who were standing nearby. J. J. motioned for them to continue. Shumway turned back toward Martha. "What happened next," he asked. Martha replied, "I said, 'Hold on, now,' and I turned her over and I killed her, and she did not kill me."

Loranger had told both doctors about the axe and the manner of the old woman's death.

"Did you strike her with an axe," Shumway asked. She answered, "I don't know, I might. I killed her anyway, and then I got on her with my feet and jumped on her as hard as I could; yes, I did. My mother told me to kill her," she continued.[29]

Martha Haney's mother, Susan Pierce, had died seven years before in Ionia, and it was rumored among the townsfolk in Williamston that Martha frequently spoke with her dead mother. In order to make a determination about her sanity, Shumway and Shaw knew they would have to question Martha about conversations with her dead mother. Both doctors had seen Martha wandering about town on previous occasions, talking to someone, or thing, unseen. Still, they weren't prepared to hear her explanation.

"Did she talk to you this morning," asked Doc Shumway. "Oh," she said in a whisper, "she comes to me every once in a while. She has been talking a great deal lately." The doctor repeated his question. "Yes, yes," Martha answered quickly, "she was talking to me all the while. She told me to kill the old lady, or she would kill me. I told her I did not want to kill her, but she kept saying, 'kill her', so I killed her."[30]

Shumway and Shaw nodded to one another then turned toward J. J. They concurred the woman was insane but had learned very little about how the deed had been done.[31] Like the doctors, the sheriff and his deputy walked out of the building and could hear the murderess crying in the cell behind them.

Doc Shumway quickly offered to assist in the matter by providing his professional opinion. J. J. quickly accepted the offer. The sheriff knew that if he was going to pursue the criminal process, he needed doctors' opinions. Dr. Shaw also offered his services for any upcoming hearings regarding Martha's state of mind. Knowing that Justice McEnally was on his way, J. J. assured the physicians that should he need anything further, he would certainly summon them. He knew that he wouldn't have to address the woman's mental state at this point, but only show there had been a killing and that Martha Haney had confessed to it. The doctors' opinions would be needed later should the matter proceed to trial.

Doc Shumway took a cigar from his coat pocket, struck a match, lifted it and slowly inhaled. The end of the cigar glowed bright red and soft smoke slowly curled around the doctor's head in the cool air. He asked if the sheriff needed anything else. J. J. shook his head and extended his hand as a thank you to both men, telling them he may need them to testify later.

As the physicians turned and walked back to the Plank Road, J. J. told Deputy Whitehead to keep a close eye on their prisoner.

As Whitehead headed toward the calaboose, J. J. walked toward the center of the village along the Plank Road. Half a block down, he stopped at a general store and bought a cigar. After seeing the old woman's body, with her head severed and served as a table centerpiece, surrounded by the acrid odor of her own seared flesh, J. J. had thoroughly welcomed the smell of Doc Shumway's cigar. He decided then and there to purchase one of his own. Stepping out of the store and into the afternoon gloom, he struck a match on one of his buttons, lit the cheroot and walked back toward the village hall. He contemplated his next step as he inhaled the rich aroma of burning tobacco.

The village was abuzz with word of the crime, and as the sheriff approached the hall, he noticed a small group of townsfolk standing in front of the Opera House just to east. They intently eyed his every step. J. J. ignored them and headed up the small driveway leading to garage.

Whitehead greeted him near the front of the fire engine. He reported that the prisoner had continued to cry but seemed otherwise under control. J. J. looked beyond his deputy to the cell. Martha was still sitting on the floor, her head hung low, her hands clasped behind her head as if trying to protect herself from something falling from heaven. J. J. told Whitehead that Justice McEnally didn't live far, and it shouldn't take him too long to arrive for the inquest. In the meantime, they would simply have to wait for his arrival.

J. J. expected Loranger would be bringing the murderess' husband to the village hall soon. He wondered out loud what the man's name was. Whitehead told him Martha's husband's name was Alfred, but everyone called him Alfy. J. J. took the pocket watch from his pocket and checked the time. He and his prisoner would need to be on the 7:00 p.m. train.

While J. J. and Whitehead were waiting for Justice McEnally, Undertaker Fred Rockwell waited to begin his awful task. Mariah Haney's body would be placed inside the wooden coffin. There was little new about that. But this time Rockwell would have to lift the gruesome centerpiece from the dining table and lay the deceased's head in the coffin next to the body. He knew there was no way to make this look right. Normally, Rockwell would display a corpse in a suitable home after carefully preparing the body for burial. The cooling board he typically used to preserve the recently departed for a few days during viewings would be of no use this time. Mariah Haney's remains could never be reassembled sufficiently to allow for a viewing. Given the viciousness of the attack, he could only put the old woman in her coffin and nail it shut.

Knowing the Haneys had been supported by the village over the past winter, and given their wretched living conditions, he also knew that Mariah's son, Alfy, likely wouldn't be able to afford the $110 required for a proper casket and service.

While Rockwell was still waiting at the Haney house, Loranger had located the killer's husband. Alfy Haney was a man of slight stature. When Loranger found him, he was wearing denim pants with side suspenders stretched over a filthy white shirt.

Alfy's friends had taken him in after his mother's ravaged body was found. To no one's surprise, Haney and his well-meaning sympathizers all ended up at the local saloon. Inside the tavern, three billiard tables lined one side of the large room with a bar spanning the opposite wall. Toward the rear of the room was a large, glass showcase displaying several boxes of cigars.

Alfy, although distraught, actually began to enjoy his newfound celebrity as others in the saloon bought him beer in an effort to numb the effects of what he had just seen.

Loranger, hearing that Alfy had ended up at the saloon, headed there himself. Spotting Haney surrounded by other patrons, the deputy made his way toward the bar and told Alfy the sheriff would want to talk to him. Alfy, his eyes watering, nodded, lifted his glass in a most determined way, finished the last swill of beer, and stood up. He walked solemnly to the door with Loranger. They got into the deputy's buggy and headed back to the village hall just two blocks east.

J. J. saw Loranger and Haney as they approached. He walked down the short driveway to greet them near the hitching post. Better to stop them there, he thought, than to have Alfy enter the lock-up unprepared and see his wretched wife caged like an animal. He extended his hand in sympathy to Haney, offering condolences about the man's mother. Alfy, having consumed a few too many beers, broke down in tears. J. J. stood there for an awkward moment letting him mourn. Then he told Alfy he would need to talk to him about his mother and his wife.

J. J., Loranger and Haney walked toward the building, but this time, instead of entering the garage, J. J. steered them to the offices at the east end of the village hall.

As the late afternoon wore on, Alfy willingly shared the information needed by the sheriff to proceed with the impending inquest. The sheriff and deputy listened intently as he detailed his tumultuous relationship with his wife.

Alfy married Martha Woodard in 1894. Martha was one of seven children raised on the Pierce farm a few miles to the south and west of the village on Linn Road west of Zimmer Road. Her brother, Richard, lived in Mason while another brother, William, 23 years her senior, lived in Lansing. Siblings George, Esther and Florence had all married and started families of their own. The youngest brother of the family, Otie, never lived to see the age of 13.

In 1884 she married a man named John Woodard.[32] Martha was just 16 years old. Woodard was five years her senior. Together they had three children, but Woodard eventually abandoned her. J. J. asked about the children, but Alfy had no idea where they were. She didn't have the children when he married her, Alfy explained, and he just figured that Woodard had taken them with him when he left her. Alfy had never asked Martha where the children were. Her volunteered story about their whereabouts raised a doubt in his mind, especially with regard to the youngest. She told him that of the three children, the oldest boy was living in Ohio, and the girl was living in Pennsylvania. It was the third and youngest child Alfy had quietly wondered about. Still, his curiosity never caused him to inquire.

It was said that about eight years prior, while she was living with her aged parents, she took her third and youngest child, a son, and set off on foot toward Lansing. After a day or two, she returned without the child, who had apparently been just old enough to sit up. When Martha was asked where the child was, she said she gave the boy away. Alfy now wondered, as did many of the townsfolk, if the child might have come to a much different fate.[33] But while Alfy and the entire town may have wondered about the fate of Martha's youngest child, on May 6, 1897, the Ingham County News reported: "Any suspicion that Martha Haney ever currently disposed of her child while living in Wheatfield several years ago is all wrong. She did the best of it, and placed it in charge of Rev. W. S. Sly of Lansing, the gentleman who has done such an excellent work with homeless children."[34]

Born in 1848, Reverend Winfield S. Sly was the son of a state senator and founder of the Rocky Beach Benevolent Association. He became an ordained minister in 1869. The Association's sole purpose was placing orphaned or indigent children in private homes. A focal point of the Rocky Beach Benevolent Association was it's monthly magazine, titled *The Orphan's Voice*. Reverend Sly edited this publication and enjoyed this work more than anything. He began the Association in 1888 while living in Lansing.

Funding for the Rocky Beach Benevolent Association was provided through free-will donations. The children in its charge were kept in private homes in Lansing until more permanent settings could be located for them. Advisory boards set up in local rural school districts, the superintendents of those districts, wards in participating municipalities, received and collected money. They also choose those families with which to place children for adoption. A report was then made to the general manager of the Association. Great care was always taken in selecting prospective adoptive parents and the homes into which children were eventually placed.

There could be no doubt that Reverend Sly had a loving heart for orphans. He had married Maggie Woolworth, who was herself an orphan.

It was late June in 1891 when Martha Haney met Reverend Sly. With her youngest son, at only ten months old, held in her arms, she travelled to Lansing with her sister, Florence Strong. Florence knew there was no way Martha could care for another child. Her two older children, Emily and Ernest, had already been given up for adoption. Florence knew, given Martha's condition, that this would be the best thing for young George.

At only 25 pounds, George was as cute as any baby his age. Favored with light colored hair, dark eyes and a light complexion, he had an infectious smile to warm any heart.

Arriving at the Rocky Beach Benevolent Association in Lansing's 600 block of East Michigan Avenue, Martha and Florence were met by Reverend and Mrs. Sly. Martha's ability to read and write was limited at best, so the Application for Admission to The Care of Rocky Beach Benevolent Association was filled out by her sister. In one of the last sections of the two-page application, line 28 read:

> I hereby resign and convey to the Rocky Beach Benevolent Association all rights and control that have heretofore existed between me and George Alfred Woodard.

The application was signed by Martha, and witnessed by Florence, along with Mrs. P. Husted.[35]

After learning of the good work that Reverend Sly did with orphaned children throughout Michigan, and indeed the entire country, suspicion about Martha taking the life of her own children subsided. The townsfolk realized that Martha had likely had turned over all three of her children to the minister before she and Alfy ever met.

After Alfy married Martha, the couple settled in Leroy Township with his mother, Mariah. Mariah and her husband John had been among the original settlers of the Township. John, a civil war veteran, had passed away in 1872. Mariah was now in her eighties and, even with Alfy's assistance, was unable to continue with the family farm. Alfy told J. J. that he and his bride, along with his mother Mariah, moved to the bleak cottage near the railroad in Williamston hoping to find work. The Sheriff listened intently as Haney continued.

Alfy told J. J. that during the winter months it was hard to find work, and Martha had been in poor health. He described their home as cheerless. They had been supported through most of the winter by the village.[36]

Alfy didn't know too much about Martha's parents, only that her father was elderly. Her original name had been Martha Pierce, and he knew she had at least one brother named Richard, along with some other brothers and sisters. He told J. J. that her mother had died in Ionia around 1890. J. J. made a mental note of that, knowing that the Asylum for the Criminally Insane was in Ionia. He couldn't help but wonder if Martha's mother had died there. He thought to himself that the location of her death could simply be a coincidence. He fully suspected, however, that daughter Martha would likely end up there.

Pressing on, J. J. asked for details about what had happened that very day. Alfy's eyes began to swell with tears and his chest began to heave. The stale odor of beer on his breath pervaded the small room as Alfy began to describe the day.

In painstaking detail he told of his discussion with Doc Shumway the day before and how he had planned to have Shumway talk to Martha. He described his wife's demeanor on this morning and how he had not forced the issue when she had said she felt fine. He decided it wouldn't hurt to wait just one more day, a Saturday, and not risk missing a day's wages. At the end of his narrative, Alfy described his sheer horror upon walking into the house and discovering his mother's decapitated body on the floor, her mutilated head set on the table staring at his place setting.

Finished with Alfy, J. J. turned his attention to making arrangements for Martha's transportation to the Ingham County Jail in Mason.

That night, Alfy Haney wandered the streets of Williamston sharing his incredible story with anyone willing to stop long enough to listen.[37]

THE AWFUL DEED

Alfy had known something was wrong for a very long time. So did many townsfolk in the small village of Williamston.

There were many times he had heard his wife talking to no one in particular in an otherwise empty room. From all appearances she was having a conversation with someone, or something, unseen. But to Alfy it wasn't just that. He and Martha married in 1894, and it wasn't long after their marriage when he realized there was something peculiar about his new bride. Her odd conversations with no one became more frequent. Alfy had been told she was prone to epileptic fits when she had been younger, though he had never witnessed any. And then there was her temper. He hated how it seemed to escalate quickly to a boiling point. More than once they had quarreled to the point where he almost had to lay hands on her.

Alfy was a street laborer who found work wherever and whenever it was offered. He tried hard to support his wife and mother, who had moved into the house with them, but mostly they depended on the generosity of the village. The only house they could afford sat east of the stave mill, in the constant din of the mill and several trains that rumbled through daily.

Alfy's mother Mariah never liked Martha. At 85 she was now a frail old woman, having been worn down by living on a farm for the majority of her 80-plus years. She and her husband had been among the first settlers in Ingham County's Leroy Township. Mariah's husband John died over 20 years ago, leaving her to raise Alfy, his brother Riley, and their sister, Louisey. A civil war veteran, John was buried in Rowley cemetery between Williamston and Webberville. After John's death the family lived near the Plank Road west of the village, before later moving in with another family east of the village.

From the first day she met her Mariah knew there was something different about Martha. She tried to convince her son not to marry the woman. She had seen Martha occasionally talking to herself, but it wasn't just that. There was something else. She just couldn't put her finger on it. Alfy's mother and wife fought often about small things. Occasionally their words turned to pushing, but neither woman ever struck the other. If there had ever been any physical altercation, Alfy never knew about it. As slight as Martha was, Mariah was even smaller.

Mariah tried to talk to her son about her daughter-in-law's instability on more than one occasion, but Alfy chose to ignore his mother's observations and comments regarding his bride. He knew his mother was right because he had seen the same things. Still, he thought if he ignored the problem maybe it would go away. Either that or they would simply get used to it.

Alfy was wrong. The last three weeks had been difficult. Now the strange, one-sided conversations were an everyday occurrence. And Martha's temper seemed to be getting worse. Alfy was becoming more concerned, and while he wasn't exactly sure why, his biggest fear was leaving his mother alone with his wife.

It was early April when Alfy had finally found some work doing street repairs for the village. The winter months had passed and the warmth of the spring sun had started to thaw the roads. The job was new and might not last very long, but any day he could earn a wage was a good day. It was physically demanding, but Alfy enjoyed working and it offered the added benefit of keeping him away from the constant bickering between his mother and his wife. One day while he was enjoying the spring temperatures near the downtown, he saw Dr. Shumway walking toward his office. As the doc passed, Alfy spoke up, asking if the doctor could spare a minute to speak with him. The doctor paused. Alfy explained his wife's peculiar behavior to the local physician. He described her conversations with no one in particular. The doctor listened intently. Clearly it sounded like the woman was suffering from some sort of madness. The doctor expected as much; on previous occasions, he had seen Martha walking about the village talking to herself. He had even heard her singing religious songs at the most inappropriate times.

It was clear to the doctor that Alfy was at a loss and didn't know what to do. He was no doubt at wits end. Dr. Shumway assured him that if he would bring his wife to the doctor's office, he would take a few minutes to speak with her. Alfy was encouraged by the doctor's consideration, yet he knew he didn't have any money to pay for the visit. More than that, he would have to find a way to convince Martha to go see the physician. He figured the money issue would be the least of his worries at this point.

As Alfy walked into the shack he called a home, he could smell something cooking on the stove. It was cabbage. Martha was in the back yard. She was staring at nothing in particular…just staring. While his mother stirred the contents of the cast iron pot, Alfy took advantage of their moment alone and told Mariah he had talked to Doc Shumway. She gave him a worried look and wondered out loud how Alfy could convince Martha to go. He assured his mother it wouldn't be a problem. That was probably untrue. But he knew something had to be done. It would cost him a day's wage, but it would be worth it.

Alfy looked out the back door. Martha was still staring blankly. Occasionally she spoke, but no one was there. After watching her for several minutes, Alfy startled his wife by yelling her name and calling her inside for supper.

The three sat at the kitchen table. The stove was packed with freshly chopped wood in an effort to warm the tiny house. More wood sat on the floor next to the stove. Plates were stacked to one side of the table from the previous night's supper still caked with dried food. The old wooden chair Alfy sat on creaked as he stood up. He walked toward the living room. Making it appear as an afterthought, yet intentionally, he told Martha that he had spoken with Doc Shumway and he was going to take her to see the doc tomorrow morning in hopes of finding out what was ailing her. Martha, who had been staring at her plate, looked up at Alfy, then at Mariah, then back at Alfy. Becoming belligerent, she insisted there was nothing wrong with her. As Alfy sat down in the dimly lit room adjacent to the kitchen, the soft glow of an oil lamp on the wall highlighted the shadow of his three-day growth of beard. He told her they would let the Doc decide that.

Panic set in...sheer terror. Martha's mind began to race. Suddenly she felt even colder than she already was. She tightened the shawl draped over her shoulders. Careful not to look at her daughter-in-law, Mariah got up and quietly walked to the bedroom just off the kitchen. Warily she waited for Martha to react, but Martha only sat and stared at her plate. Her warmed cabbage turned cold. She sat for a very long time.

Alfy finished a cigar and headed toward the bedroom off the living room when Martha finally rose from the table. She walked to the living room. *It's not my fault! It's the old woman's fault!* She walked toward the bedroom where Alfy had just retired. In a loud voice, she told him she wanted his mother out of the house. Alfy looked at her with a puzzled look on his face. Then it dawned on him: Martha was trying to place blame on his mother as though it had been her idea to get Doc Shumway involved. Alfy told her that it wasn't about his mother. But Martha's tone grew louder. Again she insisted that she wanted the old woman out. Alfy would have no part of it. He turned his back to wife, rolling over on the bed and pulling the quilt up to his shoulders.

Martha stared at Alfy for what seemed an eternity, at least it did to Alfy, for he could feel her gaze cutting through him. He was not going to compromise. Martha was going to see Doc Shumway in the morning whether she wanted to or not. Despite her long, impenetrable stare Martha realized she wasn't going to win the battle. She turned back toward the sparsely furnished living room.

Martha lay down on the hard floor, staring into space. Sporadic sleep finally came. The thin piece of carpet covering the floor offered little warmth between the frigid wood underneath and her already shivering body.

Alfy couldn't sleep, his body rolled from one side to the other for the entire night. It wasn't because of his wife's absence. He was used to Martha sleeping in the other room. That had become common. But his mind raced with so many thoughts: *Would she go willingly? Could he afford to miss a day's pay? How long would the street work last? What's wrong with my wife? Why did I ever marry her? And what really happened to her three kids?*

Sleep finally came around 2:30 AM. He woke at 6:40. For a very brief moment he had forgotten about the previous night's conversation. However, as he sat up it all came back in a rush. Again he worried about how he would pay the doctor. He really needed the money he could earn today, but Martha also really needed to see Doc Shumway. He pulled on the same York denim apron overalls he had worn for the last four days. He had slept in the dirty white shirt from yesterday in an effort to stay warm, and he figured it was good enough for one more day. He slid on his worn Lumberman's boots and laced them up. Then Alfy walked from the bedroom into the living room. Martha wasn't there. He heard movement in the kitchen. As he walked into that room, he saw his wife bending over in front of the stove. She laid a split piece of oak on the fire, and moved the coals around to stoke glowing embers. Alfy hesitated, took a deep breath, then reminded her of their planned trip.

Martha turned from the stove with a slight smile on her face. Looking Alfy directly in the eyes, she assured him there was no reason to see Doc Shumway because she was feeling much better than she had the previous day. Alfy hadn't seen her smile for a very long time. He had forgotten what she looked like with a smile on her face. He tilted his head ever so slightly, wondering. She reminded her husband that they really needed the day's wage, telling him they could go see Doc Shumway tomorrow. She promised Alfy she would go then. Alfy knew she was right about one thing: They certainly did need the money, and Martha did seem much better this morning...better than she had been in a very long time.

Alfy still wasn't totally convinced, though, and he thought about it for a long moment. He heard his mother getting around in the bedroom off the kitchen. As Mariah entered the kitchen, she paused when she saw the grin on Martha's face. She instinctively knew something wasn't right.

Alfy thought about it again and finally agreed to his wife's proposal. What difference would one more day make? He would see Doc Shumway walking about the village that day as he did every day, and he'd tell him they would drop by tomorrow. It wouldn't make a difference that it would be Saturday. Doc Shumway, like any good country doctor, would see anyone whenever they had the need... even on weekends.

Alfy turned toward his mother and briefly told her of the change in plans. He didn't elaborate. He crossed the room, grabbed an apple from the counter and was out the door. It was almost a relief that he wouldn't have to take Martha today. Putting it off for one more day came as a pleasant relief to him. When Alfy left the house, Martha's smile broadened. She had done it. She told Alfy she was feeling better, and to go ahead and go to work.[38] He had bought the lie.

It was only a facade of sanity. Martha had lain on the cold floor all night wrapped in a shawl, contemplating her next move between short bouts of sleep. If she saw the doctor, he would surely question her reasoning. But that was foolish. *There's nothing wrong with you,* her mother had told her many times. Yes, she had spoken with her mother many times, and while others didn't believe it, she knew the truth. She conversed on a regular basis with the deceased woman. In fact, as she shivered on the floor the previous evening, the two women talked a great deal about what needed to be done.

Her conversations with her dead mother had gone on for several months. Everyone in the village knew it. She didn't mind that people knew, or even that some thought she was daft. She knew the only way to postpone her eventual examination by the doc would be to control her fury and deceive her husband. She would start in the morning. It would be a difficult task, but she was sure if she could just control her anger she could convince Alfy to go work on the streets. Then she would have another day.

After Alfy's departure, she glanced at her mother-in-law. Mariah, still leery of Martha's sudden personality change, broke the awkward silence telling Martha she was going to start cleaning up. Martha, anxious and trying not to tip off the old woman, agreed to help.

The morning of April 23, 1897 dawned like any other Mid-Michigan spring day as Alfy headed toward downtown. The clouds overhead would surely open up and drench the village as he walked west toward Putnam Street. After passing VanBuren's Cold Storage and J. W. Linn's Elevator, he glanced at the depot to his right. The first passengers of the day were already waiting for the morning train. He continued on, crossing the tracks and heading south toward the center of the village.

Next to the Haney house, the Williamston Stave Company was in full operation. The narrow-shaped pieces of wood used to form the sides of oak barrels were a large commodity. Sometimes the Williamston Stave Company produced as many as 6,000,000 staves per year. Most were sent to Chicago, some to St. Louis. In addition to the staves, packing barrels were another of the company's products, and the demand for those products made it one of the biggest businesses in the village.[39] The manufacturing company had been started by James Schultz in Lansing in 1869. The worldwide need for staves had increased rapidly over recent years as meats, cider, vinegar, pickles and other foods were packed into oak barrels and casks. The seemingly endless demand resulted in Schultz opening factories in Williamston and Webberville, in addition to his Lansing plant.

Charles Goyt lived near the corner of Leisha Street and Railroad Street. Residing with his brother Will, he was completely unaware of what he was about to witness.

John Robinson and Will Wygant worked at the stave mill, along with a host of other townsfolk. Most of the workers at the mill had come to know the Haneys, in part because of their proximity to the mill. An occasional nod, or "good morning" was commonplace, as Alfy would pass by. Like Charlie Goyt, Robinson and Wygant were about to experience something they would never forget.

While Robinson began his morning shift at the mill, in the house next door Mariah stacked dishes from the previous night on top of the already dirty dishes from two nights ago. She returned to her bedroom and got dressed as she heard Martha cleaning in the living room. Mariah took a hairbrush from atop the dresser and ran it through her gray hair. Putting her spectacles on, she walked back into the kitchen and glanced into the living room. Martha had her back to her, and it looked as though she had something in her hands, but Mariah couldn't see what it was. Ignoring her, Mariah started to move things about too, in an effort to tidy up the house.

Martha left the house through the front door. As she walked between the house and the stave mill, she raised a ladle into the air swinging it around her head while singing some spiritual song. Working nearby, Robinson glanced at her thinking Mrs. Haney was at it again.

As the morning wore on the two women continually ignored each other, much like they did every day while tending to their daily household tasks. Mariah worked both inside and out. It was no secret to anyone who lived or worked near the Haney household that the two women despised each other.

Mariah noticed that Martha had begun mumbling again. Trying to stay away from her, Mariah went out to the pump. She suspected that Martha's good nature this morning had all been a ruse. After filling a bucket with fresh water, she set it on the ground next to the pump and threw a couple rugs over a clothesline. She struck the sides of the rug with an old broom. Dust and dirt cascaded to the ground as she continued her frenzied swings. Over the noise of the broom she could hear movement from inside the house. There was a banging sound, a kind of hammering. Already suspicious of Martha's morning behavior, Mariah wondered what her daughter-in-law was up to.

Mariah removed the rugs from the clothesline and walked back into the house. As she crossed the kitchen and looked into the living room, Martha was standing very still. She was staring at a picture on the wall. Mariah paused. That picture hadn't been there earlier in the morning. Martha had her back to Mariah, and as Mariah looked over her shoulder, she recognized the picture frame. Earlier that morning it had held a photo of her husband, but now the photo was gone. In its place was a photo of three children…Martha's children. Mariah had never seen any of them, but she instantly knew those were Martha's kids.

Mariah was infuriated by her daughter-in-law's disrespect. She could no longer control her anger. Mariah took a swing at Martha with what very little strength she possessed. Her small hand landed against Martha's back, demanding to know what Martha was doing. Martha, almost instinctively, turned and gave Mariah a push. The old woman stumbled backward.

Martha began to mumble as if talking to someone else. Mariah was surprised. She had never been pushed that hard by her daughter-in-law. She didn't quite know what to think of it.

Mariah's anger escalated. She demanded to know what Martha had done with the picture of her husband. Martha simply smiled at her, asking Mariah if she thought the children were beautiful. Mariah shouted again, demanding to know where the picture of her husband was. Martha, with her glassy stare, simply responded with an eerie smile.

Next to the Haney house, the morning's work at the stave mill continued. Workers, both inside and out, were into their daily routines. Those outside could hear the arguing. They had watched the two women going about their business all morning.[40] Now the shouting had become so loud it was difficult not to notice them going at it again, as they had done so many times in the past. The workers mostly ignored the back and forth, day-to-day bickering. Occasionally they would glance at the house and smirk to themselves knowing the two women were fighting again.

As some of the mill workers watched, Martha stormed out the front door. She was mumbling, but if she intended to communicate anything, her meaning was incomprehensible. *Don't let her do this!* She stood in the front yard, glaring at the workers staring back at her from the stave mill. She slowly turned back toward the house, her steps deliberate as she reached for the front door. Martha pushed but the door didn't move. She tried again. Still the door wouldn't open. Mariah had locked it after Martha's exit.[41] Martha was enraged. *Bash it down!* She pounded on the wooden frame with her fists, screaming for Mariah to unlock the door.

Inside the house, Mariah removed the picture frame from the wall and tore out the picture of the children. She threw the picture on the floor and started to walk toward her bedroom with the frame in hand. Her body trembled from anger.

Outside the house, Martha moved quickly around toward the back, crossing between the house and the stave mill. The workers watched with great interest as Martha appeared to be searching for something in the back yard. Their interest quickly waned and they returned to their daily tasks.

It did not take long for Martha to find what she was looking for. She grabbed the axe leaning against the side of the house. She touched the edge of the blade. It was well honed and razor sharp. She stormed back around the east side to the front yard, axe in hand. Martha marched to the front door and, without a moment's hesitation, began splintering the wooden door with the axe.[42]

Mariah, now in her bedroom, put the wooden picture frame down when she heard loud crashing sounds rattling the front door. She started back toward the front room. As she hurried toward the window to see what Martha was doing, she was startled when the sharp blade from the axe bulleted through the center of the door. Shards of wood flew from the thin wooden barrier separating the two women.

Mariah froze for only a second then crouched down, raising her hands as if to protect her face. Again, and again, and again the axe splintered the door. Mariah, now in a panic, screamed as what little remained of the door finally gave way. "Murder," she yelled. Instinctively she knew Martha's intent, and it frightened her beyond anything she had ever experienced in her 85 years on this earth.

Martha stepped through the opening where the door had once been. Pieces hung on what was left of one hinge. She looked at Mariah. A mere six feet separated them.

Martha's breathing was labored now, and in spite of the cool spring temperature, beads of sweat slowly ran down her forehead. The axe had seemed so heavy when she first picked it up, but now felt as light as a down pillow. She stared at Mariah, whose old face was contorted in terror. Martha's smirk, the axe in her hand, the determination in her eyes; Mariah knew without any doubt that this would be her end. In one last hopeless attempt, knowing how unlikely it was that anyone would hear her frail voice, she again screamed, "Murder!"

Workers at the stave mill had continued about their morning labor after watching Martha storm back to the house. After all, the women's bickering and fighting was a common occurrence. They never expected it would escalate beyond the usual day-to-day shouting. But this time they hadn't seen Martha grab the axe. They knew nothing of what was about to be.

Martha's two small hands tightly gripped the axe handle now. As Mariah screamed, Martha brought the blunt side of the axe across her mother-in-law's face, knocking the old woman backward and down to the floor. Helpless, Mariah felt the weight of the blunt, cold steel strike her cheekbone, shattering it. As she stumbled and fell to the floor, she blacked out for a moment. As she regained her consciousness, the pain was excruciating. She couldn't make a sound.

Immediately after striking her first blow with the axe, Martha reversed her motion in an effort to connect with Mariah's head a second time. But Martha missed with her backhanded second swing, as Mariah had fallen backward.

Mariah lay on the floor. She tried in vein to get up, reaching for the edge of an old couch. In the chill of the room she could feel her own warm blood against the cool skin of her face as a red torrent poured from the newly inflicted gash across her cheek. She fought to regain her senses while her vision blurred. Dazed and on the floor leaning against the couch, she desperately reached for something…anything…on the floor to defend herself. The pain was unbelievable. Her already blurred vision began to fade, but through the fog of blood and agony she could still make out a dark figure moving toward her. Instinctively, she struggled to move away. Then the blunt head of the axe struck the side of her face again. Complete darkness. The attack ended, at least for a moment. Martha, swinging with all of her might, succeeded in knocking the old woman unconscious. Blood, pouring freely from Mariah's split face, pooled quickly on the floor.

Martha stopped. Her eerie grin disappeared. She stared at the bloodied, slight body of her mother-in-law now crumpled like a rag doll on the floor. She watched Mariah's labored breaths as the old woman's life began to quickly fade.

Kill her! If you don't kill her, she'll kill you! Martha could hear her own mother's voice, and she knew she was right. She knew she had to finish off the old woman. Martha's grip on the axe handle loosened. The axe dropped to the floor. With what strength she had left, Martha raised her right leg over the dying figure lying before her. In a fury, she stomped on her mother-in-law's body with her feet. She stomped again and again in a frenzy unlike any she had ever known. She could hear the old woman's ribs crack, feeling them break under the weight of her blows. *Kill her! Kill her!* Her mother's voice grew louder now, more demanding.

The old woman had barely a breath left in her. The blood collecting in the back of Mariah's throat gurgled as her labored breaths passed. Crimson colored liquid bubbled as it escaped from her slack lips.

Martha methodically surveyed the scene. As she looked around the room, she spotted the axe she had dropped. It was lying on the floor not too far away. She stared at the battered old woman. Mariah unconsciously gasped, struggling to breathe. Martha's smirk returned and the corners of her mouth slowly turned upward. She looked at the nearly lifeless body lying before her. *Kill her!*

Once again, Martha picked up the implement she had taken from the back yard and grasped the axe handle with both hands. She slowly raised it above her head. Then, calling on what remained of her strength, she brought the axe down with all of her might. The first glancing blow struck the side of Mariah's head, taking a large gouge out of her scalp. The hardened steel extracted a clump of Mariah's gray hair from her skull and embedded it with a sharp thump into the wooden floor. Martha struggled to pull the blade of the axe free from the floor. It wasn't easy, but soon the floor released its grip and the axe was freed. *Kill her!*

Martha raised the axe again. In a frenzied motion, she brought the axe down as hard as she could, cutting cleanly through Mariah's neck and severing her throat. Blood that had pooled there was released. It flowed from the open wound that stretched across the front of her neck. Martha thought Mariah might still be alive. She wasn't. Still, Martha yanked the axe blade from the wooden floor a second time. Her determination had grown to an unstoppable crescendo.

She raised the axe a final time.

The last blow severed the old woman's head completely. Martha heard an odd crackling sound as the blade sliced cleanly through the old woman's spine, splintering the bones in her neck.

It was done. Mariah's lifeless body lay in two pieces, her half-open eyes staring into blank space.

Once again, Martha yanked the axe blade from the floor. She fought to catch her rapid breaths. Her thoughts raced. She looked quickly around. *What should I do with the old woman? What if someone finds out? How dare Alfy insist I go see a doctor! There's nothing wrong with me!* She glanced down. She hadn't realized it, but Mariah's blood had spoiled her dress. She cursed her husband. *This is his fault! I'll show him!* She rested the axe against the chair Mariah's body had overturned when she fell.

Moving to the kitchen, she took a plate from the counter and set it in the middle of the table. She didn't notice the blood on her fingers smearing the edges. She took a knife and fork from the cluttered countertop and carefully placed one on each side of the plate.[43] Martha's breathing was more relaxed now. She walked back into the living room, reached down and grabbed her mother-in-law's detached head by the blood-matted gray hair. She walked back to the kitchen, leaving a trail of blood as she moved from one room to the next. Then she set the grisly centerpiece on the plate. Martha stopped for a moment to admire her handiwork. *No, that's not right.* With the old lady's blood dripping from her hands, she adjusted the gift she had prepared for her husband by turning Mariah's head so it would face Alfy's creaky old dinner chair. Then she smiled.

Staring at her accomplishment, panic slowly started to set in. The head was properly presented but that battered body in the living room just wouldn't do. Grabbing her victim's headless corpse by the feet, she dragged it to the kitchen. She started breathing harder now. The old woman was small, but her body seemed incredibly heavy as she pulled the torso through the house.

By the time she reached the back door Martha was out of breath. Her anxiety grew when she realized that she would surely be seen by the workers at the stave mill if she dragged the body outside. *Quick. Think.* But there was precious little time to think. Then it came to her: *Burn the house with the old woman inside.* Leaving the body in the kitchen, she moved to the front room. Her head darted from side to side as she searched for an oil lamp. Grabbing the first one she saw she darted back to the kitchen. Mariah's half-opened, glassy, dead eyes stared at Alfy's chair from the center of the table as Martha passed. She poured kerosene from the lamp across the headless corpse. Emptying the lamp, she threw it to the floor, then reached for a pan of shriveled potatoes lying on the counter. Throwing the potatoes on the floor, she scooped burning coals from the stove into the pan and laid the now heated metal container between the old woman's legs.

Everything was moving faster now. She had to get rid of her own clothing. *Too much blood.* Quickly unbuttoning her frock, she let it fall to the floor then threw it on her mother-in-law's decapitated body as it began to smolder. Martha turned her head, quickly taking one last glance toward the table centerpiece, almost as if to confirm the old woman was really dead. She walked quickly back to the front room and retrieved the murder weapon. As she bent forward to pick it up she noticed her children. The picture; it had looked so nice in the frame. Now that picture was spattered with blood and lying on the floor. She picked it up. Wiping away the droplets, she held the picture to her chest and then concealed it in her bosom.

Back to the kitchen. Now clad only in her Princess Union Suit Martha quickly left through the back door as smoke from the smoldering corpse began to fill the kitchen. She laid the axe under some boards beneath the rear stairs at the back of the house.[44] *Maybe they won't find it here,* she thought to herself, then: *What have I done?*

No one at the stave mill noticed.

Smoke spread slowly to the front room from the smoldering body. All of Martha's thoughts began to run together. Her mind was a blur now. Her breathing came in ragged gasps.

As Martha stood panicked at the back of the house, Alfy was approaching from the west, completely unaware of the carnage inside. He'd been working all morning without any sort of a break, and now it was lunchtime. Alfy had eaten only the apple he grabbed as he left the house that morning. As he walked toward the small house he didn't notice his wife. Before he could get to the front door, she entered from the back and slipped into Mariah's bedroom.

Alfy, his mind wandering, also didn't notice the smoke starting to seep ever so slightly from cracks around the windows of the house. His gait was steady and his hands were clasped behind his back. He slowed when he realized the door was in shreds and hanging on a single hinge. He quickly stepped closer and saw the large holes cut through the ruined door. He noticed an odor…a putrid odor…one he'd never smelled before. He saw the smoke. Then glancing quickly toward the kitchen through the smoke, he could see the gift his wife had left for him on the table. It was his mother's head! With all of his senses revolting he tried to make sense of it all.

The scream was piercing. It was unlike any scream ever heard before in the village…blood curdling. Alfy turned and ran from the house. Stumbling as he bolted, he fell. He got up and sprinted. He ran as fast as he could, crossing the tracks directly in front of the house, passing between the old fruit evaporator and a hay storage barn… running…faster and faster. Tears streaming down his face, he ran down White Street. He had to find the law.

Charlie Goyt had just left his house near the corner of Leasia Street when he heard the scream and saw Alfy running from the front door. He wondered what all the commotion was, and then noticed the smoke beginning to emanate from the front door and windows. He thought to himself, *Alfy's house is on fire!* Yelling for his brother Will, he ran toward the house thinking he might be able to extinguish any fire if it were still small enough. Now noticing the smoke, neighbor Will Wygant saw the Goyt brothers running toward the Haney house. Wygant joined them in trying to save the wooden shack.

The smoke had thickened making it difficult to see. It looked as if most of the smoke was coming from a rear window of the house near the kitchen. Goyt grabbed a bucket from the back yard. He filled the bucket as fast as he could from the pump while the other two men also grabbed buckets. One by one they started throwing pails of water through the rear window of the house. The thick smoke prevented them from seeing inside and gauging whether their efforts were doing any good. One of the men broke another window on the side of the house and started throwing water through it. As the three men continued their attempts to put out the fire, John Robinson had just walked from the mill. He saw the three men trying to extinguish the fire. He ran back to the mill, grabbed a bucket of water and he sprinted toward the front of the house.

When Robinson entered the house, he immediately smelled the odor of kerosene. He moved into the living room, not noticing the broken door on the hinge he had just passed through. Robinson could hear the other three men yelling outside, and as he got to the kitchen he saw a heap of something smoldering on the floor. He poured his bucket of water on it. He ran out the back of the house to the pump and refilled his bucket. Re-entering from the back, he poured another bucket of water on the pile. Then he stopped, trying to make sense of what was before him. He stared. The smoldering heap, now soaked with water, resembled a body….a headless body. Not believing what his eyes were trying to piece together, he turned to look around the room. His gaze stopped at the table's centerpiece. It was Mariah Haney's severed head sitting on a bloody plate with adorning silverware on either side.

As John Robinson stood in disbelief, Martha calmly walked from the bedroom. Robinson turned and saw her at the same time she saw him. Not realizing either was in the house, they startled one another. She recognized Robinson from the mill. For his part, Robinson still couldn't believe any of what he was seeing. Almost as if he wasn't there, Martha nonchalantly bent down and moved the potatoes around that were lying on the floor in a pool of Mariah's blood. Still dressed in only her drawing with a nightdress tucked into her drawers, she stood back up and returned to the bedroom.

Robinson slowly turned from watching Martha's exit and once again tried to comprehend the scene that lay before him. He stared with incredulity at the grisly setting. His gaze went from the body, to the table, and back to the body. He could see what was left of human hands protruding from the pile of burned clothing. As he tried to gather his wits, Martha emerged from the bedroom again, this time wearing a dress over her undergarments. She walked toward the living room and lay down on a lounge. She laid there only a moment then sat up. Kneeling on the lounge, she started to peel the paper from the walls of the living room.

Aware that the fire was out, the Goyt brothers and Will Wygant stood outside trying to figure out what was going on and why Robinson remained in the house. There was still considerable smoke, but they could see Robinson had extinguished whatever had been burning. As far as they knew he was the only person in the house. They were unaware that he was in the company of a killer.

There was a commotion outside as word of the fire quickly spread. Others from the mill started to come toward the house. Robinson, keeping his eyes on an insane killer trying to peel paper from the walls, slowly backed out of the house. As he did, Martha got up from the lounge and left the house through the back door. She kneeled in the yard behind the house and started digging frantically with her hands.

Once outside Robinson paused only for a moment. He knew he had to find Deputy Loranger.

It wasn't long before others in the mill and around town learned of the calamity and started making their way to house. As the curious moved in that direction, so did Loranger. Alfy had found the deputy on Middle Street just a few blocks from where his mother had been killed. Together they made their way to the house as fast as Loranger's horse and carriage would go. As they travelled south on Putnam and turned toward the train depot, Loranger could see crowds starting to gather in front of the house. He stopped near the depot, jumped off his carriage and ran to the east telling Alfy to hold the horse and carriage. As he passed the stave mill he could see Robinson motioning to him, pointing toward the back yard. He stopped and looked. There was Martha digging in the dirt with her bare hands behind the house. The two men slowly approached her.

Loranger asked Martha what was going on. She hadn't noticed the two men approaching, and Loranger's voice startled her. With a blank look on her face, she told the men she had killed her mother-in-law. She coughed softly from the smoke from the smoldering body in the house. Martha told the men the old woman was inside. Loranger took note of her blank stare and eerie grin. Both men slowly walked up to her. Robinson had seen everything, but Loranger was still in disbelief. Martha told them she had cut off the old woman's head. The lawman could smell the smoke from the house as it mixed with the odors from the stave mill.

Loranger had no doubt now that what Alfy had told him was true. He glanced quickly around for whatever Martha might have used to do the old woman in but saw nothing. The men gently grasped each arm of the murderess and slowly stood her up. Loranger took the heavy shackles he carried with him and placed them on her tiny wrists. He asked Robinson to stay with Mrs. Haney as he went inside the back of the house. Loranger exited as quickly as he had entered. Much like Robinson, the deputy felt like retching at the sights and smells of the interior. He told Robinson to enlist a couple of the men standing about and not let anyone into the house. He was going to take Martha down to the lockup then wire for the sheriff. He would be back.

THE INQUEST

J. J. knew what would be next. The law was very clear. He would first have a coroner's inquest to determine if there was enough evidence to believe a crime had been committed. He knew proof of a crime would clearly not be a problem. He was required to notify the Justice of the Peace who would preside over the hearing. Under Michigan's law, if a person came to their death suddenly or by violence, an inquest had to be held.

In order for the inquest to take place, J. J. would have to find six good and lawful men to serve as jurors. The process would probably not take long, as there could be no question in anyone's mind as to how Mariah Haney had met her demise.

J. J. knew the inquest would have to be held in the village, but specifically - and eerily - it would be held at the Haney house. Years before J. J. had ever been elected as sheriff, in a different case involving a death, an inquest had actually been held in a saloon in the small village of Dansville, south of Williamston, as that was the place where the death had occurred.

The legal instruction for the Justice of the Peace was quite clear in Martha Haney's case. Given the nature Mariah's death, the location where the juror's oath would be taken was clear:

> "...And there, in view of the dead body, shall [the Justice of the Peace] administer the oath."[45]

The six jurors would have to see the entire grisly scene, but there would be no decision as to Martha's mind-set at the time of the murder.

J. J. knew Justice of the Peace William H. McEnally personally. Justice McEnally also served as the Pension Attorney for the village. They had become acquainted over the years having both worked in service for the township and the village. J. J. asked Deputy Loranger to head down to McEnally's office and have him come directly to the village hall.

The inquest would determine if Mariah Haney had been murdered, and, if so, whether it was likely that Martha Haney had committed the crime. The inquest may have been simply a formality in this case, but it was still required by law. J. J. expected he and John Robinson would be the only people called upon to testify. Robinson, who had entered the house within minutes after the murder, would describe Martha's actions inside the house, in addition to what he had seen. Loranger, who placed the murderess under arrest, would not be needed at this point.

Williamston's Justice of the Peace arrived at the village hall shortly after being summoned by Loranger. Like J. J., he knew what his role would be this day: he would preside over an inquest where six jurors would make a determination as to whether a murder had occurred. The job would not be difficult in this instance. The jury simply had to follow the law:

> "The jury, upon inspection of the dead body, and after hearing the testimony of the witnesses, and making all needful inquiries, shall draw upon and deliver to the justice of the peace, their inquisition under their hands, in which they shall find and certify, when, in what manner, and by what means the deceased came to his death, and his name, if known, together with all the material circumstances attending his death; and if it appear that he came to his death by unlawful means, the jurors shall forthwith state who was guilty, either as principal or accessory, or were in any manner the cause of his death, if known.[46]

J. J. told Deputy William Whitehead to head downtown and round up six men to serve as jurors at the inquest. Knowing how grisly the inside of the house was, J. J. instructed Whitehead to make sure that whoever he chose had a strong stomach.

J. J. left Loranger at the lockup with the murderess, then he and

Justice McEnally took Loranger's carriage and headed back toward the Haney house. As they turned the carriage onto the un-named street leading to the feed and grain elevator, they noticed the crowd still standing around despite the cool spring shower and occasional soft-rolling thunder. Undertaker Fred Rockwell was there, waiting patiently.

As they stopped in front of the Haney house, the sheriff and justice of the peace talked quietly, waiting for Whitehead to show up with the six jurors. It wasn't long before they saw the men approaching.

As the citizens grouped in front of the house, Justice McEnally took control of the situation, explaining that those selected would be part of a coroner's inquest into the death of Mariah Haney. He also explained that the body remained inside the house and that they should prepare themselves for a most gruesome sight.

The men glanced at one another wondering what they had gotten themselves into by volunteering for such duty. McEnally asked them to affirm their willingness to take part in the inquest. The group nodded in unison but no one uttered a sound.

The Justice then directed all the men to raise their right hand, as he administered the required oath. In a slow and serious tone he carefully pronounced each word:

> "You do solemnly swear, that you will diligently inquire, in behalf of the people of this state, when, in what manner, and by what means, the person whose body lies here dead, came to his death, and that you will make a true inquest thereof, according to your knowledge and such evidence as shall be laid before you."[47]

The men responded in unison: "I do."

Justice McEnally called the proceedings to order as the men stepped past the threshold and into hell. He explained the purpose of the hearing was not to decide if the one in custody was innocent or guilty, but only to determine if a crime had been committed and whether or not there was enough evidence to believe that she had committed it.

As expected by law, Justice McEnally assigned a scribe to record the inquest proceedings in writing.

After all the preliminary requirements were satisfied, the six jurors stood shoulder to shoulder in the cramped living room. They did their best to breathe through their mouths rather than their noses because the smell of death was overwhelming and almost too much to bear. Sheriff Rehle, McEnally, Robinson and the scribe stood before them.

McEnally called John Robinson as the first witness. Knowing he would be needed as part of the proceeding, Robinson hadn't bothered to return to the stave mill after making his discovery. Instead, he had waited patiently outside the house for J. J. and the Justice of the Peace to arrive, occasionally describing to friends what he had just seen.

Robinson addressed the jurors, first detailing his Friday morning at the stave mill. Then he told those gathered around him that he knew of the Haneys and had seen them at the house many times. He had often watched Martha and her mother-in-law bicker and argue, especially after Alfy left. After having observed Martha on many occasions, he believed she was insane.

Robinson painstakingly described how, after seeing smoke pouring from the house, he had rushed in and thrown water on what he thought was simply a pile of smoldering clothes. It was only after the pile had been extinguished that he had seen the body. He described Mariah's head carefully positioned on a dinner plate, bruised and covered in blood. He detailed Martha's actions; coming from the bedroom clothed only in undergarments, going back into the bedroom, and finally coming out with a dress on. Then he described her trying to peel paper from the walls in the living room. When asked about Martha digging in the yard behind the house, Robinson said that after having time to think about what he had seen, he assumed Martha was going to try and bury Mariah's body.

Robinson hesitated. The enormity of what had see that day began to wash over him like a giant wave. He swallowed hard. It felt as though a rock was lodged in his throat. He swallowed again, regaining his composure. He told of how it seemed to take too long for the law to arrive, and when Loranger finally did get there, he described how nervous he was as they both approached Martha.

Robinson hesitated again. After a long pause, Justice McEnally broke the silence. He asked the witness if she had said anything. There was no response. The Justice pressed him further.

Tears streamed down John Robinson's face, but he had already begun to regain his composure. He cleared his throat and prepared to tell the Justice and the jurors exactly what Martha had said. In anticipation, some of the jurors stared at the scene that lay before them, others looked away, or at the floor, but there was no way to ignore the smeared trail of blood.

Everyone knew what the witness was about to say; the truth would come as no surprise. The jurors stood in the midst of a horrendous crime scene. Even the least capable among them could observe the same things that Robinson had first seen. All were fully aware that Martha had done the killing. Justice McEnally continued his questioning, asking if Martha had detailed how she had killed her mother-in-law.

Robinson, now fully in control of his emotions, quickly told the men that Martha said she had chopped off Mariah's head. The witness' voice dropped to almost a whisper as he spoke. The Justice, wanting to make sure that all those gathered heard exactly what was said, asked him to repeat it. Speaking louder now, and without any hesitation, John Robinson testified that Martha Haney had told both him and Deputy Loranger that she had chopped off her mother-in-law's head.

The Justice thanked Robinson and discharged him as a witness. Sheriff Rehle would be the next to describe the carnage and the details of his involvement.

J. J. told of the wire he received from Deputy Loranger who had been working in Williamston that day. He recounted his meeting with the deputy at the depot and his walk to the house. He described in vivid detail the site of Mariah's smoldering, headless corpse on the kitchen floor, and he pointed to the charred remains still lying in front of the jurors. It wasn't necessary to describe the stench that permeated the small structure when he arrived because the house still reeked.

The sheriff described the table's centerpiece set neatly on a plate. He pointed toward the unbelievable sight. Staring incredulously at Mariah's mutilated head, all six jurors felt it was as though she was watching their every move. Her dull eyes remained slightly open, frozen in time. J. J. also described finding the instrument-of-death hidden behind some boards under the rear stoop.

By the time the sheriff finished his testimony, if there had been any doubt in anyone's mind as to how the killing occurred, that doubt had disappeared. The jurors conferred quietly with one another and came to a unanimous conclusion. They relayed their findings to Justice McEnally. After receiving their verdict, the Justice ruled that not only had a murder been committed, but the means of Mariah's death had been clearly established, and there was no doubt that Martha had committed it. He then told the sheriff that Martha Haney was to remain in his custody until a determination could be made regarding her state of mind.

All six jurors were then dismissed.

The rain had stopped, and the crowd outside had thinned. The evening was fast approaching. Undertaker Fred Rockwell was still waiting. As the jurors dispersed, softly whispering to their friends, Rockwell walked toward the front of the house. There, he was met by J. J. and McEnally. J. J. told him he was now free to remove Mariah's remains. Robinson stood just inside the door and offered Rockwell assistance in removing Mariah's body. Both men walked back toward the funeral carriage, removed the coffin and carried it into the house.

J. J. and Justice McEnally left, heading back toward the village hall. With the coroner's inquest behind them, J. J. would transport the murderess to the Ingham County Jail in Mason. On Monday he would make a formal complaint and obtain a warrant against her.

Neither the sheriff nor the justice spoke. Both were still struggling to comprehend the vicious murder that had occurred. J. J. knew there would probably be no trial, and Martha Haney would likely be sent to the asylum in Ionia. But there was still some question in his mind. If she was sent to the asylum, would she recover her mental capacity and then be allowed to go free? It had happened before.

J. J. recalled the case of a woman by the name of Minnie Herre. Herre had killed her own son, and a jury found her to be insane at the time of the killing. Based on their finding, she was acquitted of the murder. Minnie was sent to the Asylum for the Dangerous and Criminally Insane in Ionia and, over time, it was said she fully recovered. If J. J. recalled correctly, he had heard she was cooking at a hotel in Jackson and was said to be as sane as anyone. He wondered if Herre had been truly insane when she killed her son. Regardless, there was no doubt in his mind about Martha.

THE JAIL

The train's whistle cut through the hushed whispers of the onlookers near the house. It was 7:00 p.m., and nightfall was fast approaching as J. J. left the village lockup with his prisoner. It was the last quarter moon of the month. Deputy Loranger accompanied them both to the depot, as he would go with J. J. and Martha back to the county jail in Mason. This would likely be the last train of the day from Williamston to Lansing, so Loranger expected to spend the night in Mason at the jail. Upon their arrival in Lansing, they would board a southbound train to the county seat.

Fred Rockwell had done the best he could to clean up the Haney house. With the help of John Robinson, he tried to mop up the mess in both the front room and the kitchen. It was to no avail. Although they were less obvious, blood stains still covered both rooms. The stench from the burning body permeated everything in the home, and it remained overwhelming. The table where Mariah's head had been placed was taken from the house and burned. The plate, knife and fork were discarded. Rockwell wrapped what was left of Mariah tightly in a blanket, including her head. He and Robinson lifted the charred body and placed it inside the coffin. The simple wooden box, with Mariah's grisly remains inside, was the last thing removed from the house.

The different varieties of wood used in manufacturing coffins often reflected the economic status of the deceased. Mariah's coffin was made of simple pine.

In a typical situation, Fred Rockwell would have left the deceased loved one in the home on display for the grieving family, and they would have taken responsibility for preparing the body for a funeral. The room where the body laid would be draped in black, including black veils across the doorway. A cooling board would be used to slow decomposition prior to burial. The cooling board, a concave, metal, ice-filled chest placed over the torso of the body, was equipped with a lid, spigot and handles and constructed of zinc and wood. Responsibility for providing the ice and changing it fell upon the undertaker. It was economical, portable, and could be used after the deceased had been dressed.

This was not a typical situation. Mariah Haney's death was different. With her body in two pieces, and portions of the lower half burned almost beyond recognition, there was no way the remains could be displayed in the house. Beyond the condition of the body, the house would be a gruesome reminder of the horror that had befallen Mariah. Instead, the undertaker would remove Mariah's body to his furniture store and funeral parlor. Her coffin would be taken to the Baptist church on Cedar Street the following morning for the funeral.

The Baptist Church, Location of Mariah Haney's Funeral, Courtesy Williamston Depot Museum and Cloyce Odell

The simple pine box was loaded into Rockwell's Merts and Riddle horse-drawn hearse. This funeral car, used to transport the deceased to their final resting place, was elegant in its appearance. The glass along the sides, 40 by 84 inches, was of the finest French quality with beveled edges along the front and back. It had beautiful black, Lambrequin curtains trimmed with heavy black worsted fringe and tassels. The inside rails were silver plated and polished. The lamps on the carriage were also silver plated, ornate and made of the best materials. There were hand-carved, beautifully crafted pillars on each corner of the coach.

On Saturday, Alfy, his brother Riley and sister Louisey would mourn the loss of their mother. They would be joined by a shaken community.

As the train departed Williamston for Lansing, J. J. and Loranger settled in the passenger car on either side of the young Martha. After making the switch in Lansing, they travelled south toward Mason. A crossing watchman stood near the tracks as the 8203, a Schenectady-built Class F-81 steam engine with a coal tender and two passenger cars pulled into the Michigan Central Mason Depot at around 8:45 p.m. The lawmen disembarked and ferried their passenger to the Ingham County Jail on East Maple Street.

After the incorporation of Ingham County in 1838, it had taken ten years before the first jail was built. The first courthouse had been constructed eight years earlier. During the years without a jail, convicted and sentenced prisoners had to be taken by horse and buggy to Jackson. The first jail was built at a cost of $33. Logs were used to form cells inside the brick structure at 125 East Oak Street. The logs were placed much like a stockade fence to secure prisoners.

In 1866, long before J. J.'s tenure as the county sheriff, one incident at the county jail eventually led to a newer, more secure jail.

Then Sheriff Fred Moody had come to Michigan in the fall of 1855 and had settled in Leslie Township. He became a hotelkeeper in 1856, and in 1863 he was elected as the Ingham County Sheriff.

While Moody was in office, John Taylor, a sixteen-year-old former slave from Kentucky was taken by a mob at gunpoint. The crowd took the man to the intersection of Mason and North Street where he was lynched. He had been accused in an alleged murderous assault on the family of Daniel Buck in Delhi Township south of Mason. Sadly, it was later determined there had been no murder, only a minor assault.

Taylor had befriended Michigan civil war troops returning to the Lansing area and was considered a camp follower. Camp followers were dependent upon the charity of others. The followers, both black and white, believed people of the North should support them. From their point of view they were entitled to homes, clothing and food for having served either in the army or as slaves.

In an effort to rid themselves of their camp follower, the civil war soldiers comprising the Lansing Company told Taylor to go find work.

Taylor became a hired hand with the Buck family in Delhi Township. It didn't take long for Daniel Buck to learn that Taylor was lazy. Eventually he turned him out because he didn't trust Taylor around his wife, daughter, and mother-in-law. Taylor headed to the Bath area north of Lansing and took up residency with another black family. After being turned away by them, Taylor decided to return to the Buck farm to get some clothing and whatever he felt was owed to him. He armed himself with an ax.

Daniel Buck had left the house for the evening, and, at 10:00 pm, Taylor broke into the home and entered Buck's eleven-year-old daughter's room. Startled, she jumped up and somehow struck her head on the ax Taylor was carrying causing a minor wound. Abandoning his plans, Taylor decided to flee. He struggled with Buck's wife, and her mother, both of whom were also slightly injured in the fracas. Taylor managed to escape. Following Buck's return home, he and a posse headed out in pursuit of the miscreant. After his capture three hours later in Bath, Taylor was returned to Mason and jailed.

There was some concern among the community about escalating hostilities toward Taylor. Some of the locals asked Sheriff Moody to move Taylor to Jackson until his trial could be held. Moody refused and assured the concerned townsfolk that he and his deputy could provide adequate protection for the prisoner.

On August 23, 1866, three days after Taylor's capture, a large crowd, estimated by the local newspapers at 200, gathered around the jail at about 10:00 pm. They demanded that Taylor be turned over. Moody refused. The crowd knocked down the door to the jail, overpowered the Sheriff and took the prisoner to a tree near the train depot. There he was hung.

The morning following the lynching, Dr. Wing, a local physician, went to the Buck farm and discovered there had been no murders committed. The only blood actually drawn had come from a slight cut on the daughter's head. There was some effort to prosecute a few of the people involved in the lynching, but no one was ever convicted. Up to J. J.'s tenure as Ingham County Sheriff in 1897, the incident involving Taylor was the only reported lynching in the history of the Ingham County Jail.

By 1863, Mason's population had grown to over 500 people and the village included 12 stores, two hotels, one steam gristmill, two sawmills, one iron foundry and a potash factory.

The new jail, built in 1868, was a two-story brick home with the jail attached to the east side. The rapid increase in county business resulted in construction of not only a new courthouse, but the new jail with a residence for the sheriff. There were two separate entrances; one for the occupants of the home, and a second one on the east side of the home leading to the jail. There were six windows along the east side, three on each floor.

As J. J. walked into the jail with Martha in shackles, the noise seemed overwhelming. It was dark when they arrived in town, and the flicker of dimly lit windows lining the streets offered little illumination. J. J. and Loranger knew they couldn't put Martha in one of the main floor cells. Those cells held male prisoners. She would have to be taken to a second-floor cell. They climbed the stairs slowly as Martha cried quietly. J. J. opened the cell door and Loranger removed the prisoner's shackles. Martha hesitated as she looked at her new temporary home. She took a step in and let out a short gasp as the heavy iron door shut behind her. She could hear the tumbler in the lock as Loranger turned the key to secure the door.

J. J. and Loranger walked back downstairs to the first floor. Martha stood alone, almost frozen, staring at her new surroundings. Along one wall was a bunk suspended by chains from the ceiling. The blanket lying on the bunk was shredded at one corner from being chewed by mice. What one might call a mattress lay on the bunk, surely infested.

In the corner was a chamber pot. The mephitis was insufferable. Odors of stale urine and feces permeated both floors of the jail thanks to the constant influx of drunks and transients downstairs. Very few women were ever jailed on the first floor.

In one corner of Martha's tiny cell was a window covered with bars. A small table sat in the center. A rat scampered across the cell as she moved to the corner of the six-by-eight-foot box and sat down. She moved her hands to her face and lowered her head between her legs. Martha suddenly felt sick to her stomach. Her tears became steadier now.

J. J. and Loranger left the jail and walked into the sheriff's residence. Their growling stomachs reminded them they hadn't eaten all day. J. J.'s wife Sarah had anticipated that. She had a pot of beef stew warming on the wood stove in the kitchen. Both men sat at the table while Sarah dished out their supper, curious about the day's events.

Sarah shook her head in disbelief as J. J. described the killing. Watching her husband and his deputy devour their late dinner, her thoughts turned to the prisoner they had brought from Williamston. Sarah knew it was likely Martha had eaten nothing that day as well.

It was Sarah's job as the matron of the jail to serve meals to the inmates. While the other convicts had eaten long before J. J.'s arrival, she would have to feed the new prisoner. She quickly fried up a small piece of pork fat. She set it on a plate with three slices of bread. This was standard evening fare for the incarcerated. She included a small cup of tea, as she always did. Having finished their dinner, J. J. and Loranger accompanied Sarah to the second floor of the jail.

The newest resident of the Ingham County Jail was seated on the floor in her cell, wrapped in the tattered blanket. Her gaze was fixed at the floor. There were no tears now, only a blank stare.

J. J. unlocked the cell door and opened it. He and Loranger walked in with Sarah trailing behind. J. J. took the meager meal and placed it on the table. He said nothing to Martha. As they left, J. J. re-secured the iron door, and as the tumbler turned and clicked, it startled Martha again. After a quiet gasp and quick look, her gaze returned to the floor.

Normally, anything that would be referred to as lighting in the jail would have been extinguished by 8:00 o'clock, but J. J. decided to first give Martha a chance to eat her supper. After half an hour, J. J. returned to the second floor with his wife. The meal had gone untouched. J. J. and Sarah decided to leave it in the cell overnight. Maybe Martha would eat it later.

J. J. was concerned for Martha's well being. Given the gruesomeness of the crime, and her instability, he felt she might attempt to take her own life. J. J. decided he would sleep outside the cell door on a cot for the night.[48] He left the oil lamp nearby burning so he could keep an eye on her. Darkness now surrounded the young murderess, but not in the physical sense.

It was 3:00 a.m. when J. J., who had briefly nodded off, was awakened by the sound of movement in Martha's cell. He looked up to see her standing near the door. She clearly hadn't slept. Martha pleaded to go back to Williamston.[49] In order to appease her, J. J. told the woman that she could return in the morning. Martha continued to pace back and forth across the cell. J. J. had tried giving her some opiates, but the prisoner was determined not to sleep. She continued to complain saying that her head hurt. She wondered out loud if she was going to be whipped.

It wasn't long before word spread to the other inmates at the jail that there was a young killer in their midst. They had been anything but quiet when J. J. arrived with the new prisoner. There were ten male inmates and while some tried to sleep, the others talked or argued keeping the rest awake. Of the three cells on the first floor, prisoners were crammed into only two. The third cell had been converted to a water closet, and while there were plenty of disinfectants, the stench was still unbearable.

The tables in these cells served two purposes: they were used for the inmates to eat on and doubled as beds. For those too unfortunate to grab a table to sleep on, a couple of stools could serve the same purpose. Those without a table or stools had to make due by bunking on the floor. The mice and insects sharing the cold surroundings were defiant to the temporary residents.

There was a hole fashioned in the wall between the front portion of the jail and the cells. Meals for the first floor prisoners were passed through this hole in the wall. The turnkey never really worried about the inmates on the other side of the wall; they were simply drunks and transients who didn't have enough means to pay for their own upkeep. Oftentimes the residents of the Ingham County Jail claimed that they were guilty of nothing more than not having money to pay for lodging.

The coal stove on the first floor was supposed to be restocked on occasion to keep the prisoners warm. Unfortunately the turnkey often slept through this portion of his duties.

The second floor, where Martha had been taken, didn't have the luxury of a hole in the wall to feed prisoners. Meals had to be taken to the cells and handed through a larger opening between the iron slats that formed the cage.

As Martha paced in the darkness, the only light came from the small oil lamp outside the cell and a full moon high in the mid-Michigan sky. Earlier rain showers had cleared, and stars were visible to anyone who cared to look toward the sky. Martha wasn't one of them. She had finally laid on her side, having chosen the floor as her resting place for the night, just like she had done so many times at the home in Williamston. She wrapped herself in the blanket, her head resting on the wooden floor. With her eyes wide open, and in spite of the noise from the cells directly below her, she heard nothing. It was several hours before sleep came. A cold plate of untouched pork fat and bread still sat on the rickety table nearby.

Saturday morning dawned in Mason much like any other morning. With the previous day's rain long since passed, the cool April air had started to dry out the streets as the sun began to rise. It promised to be a much sunnier day than the one of the murder in Williamston.

Martha had woken frequently during the night frightened, not recognizing her surroundings. She curled up on the floor with the meager blanket trying to stay warm in the cold jail cell. Tears had streaked her gaunt face. Several times she had cried herself back to sleep during the long night while stroking the photo of her children she had concealed in her bosom. Each of her movements had alerted J. J., who was lying nearby on the cot.

The sheriff welcomed the daylight. Martha wasn't crying this morning. She sat on the floor in her cell, her head between her knees with her hands clasped behind her neck. Once the sun rose, she clearly recognized her surroundings from the previous evening. She stood and began to pace back and forth, back and forth.

At the first opportunity, J. J. thought he might try once again to speak with Martha while she was imprisoned at the jail. He didn't expect she would engage in a conversation, but he thought he should at least make the effort.

Meanwhile, Sarah had prepared the morning meal for the inmates. Three slices of bread each from a 2 ½ cent loaf, divided among four prisoners, five mealy potatoes, and a weak liquid concoction intended to pass as coffee. After having turnkey George Landenburger serve the men in the first floor cells, Sarah went to the second floor. Martha was still pacing with her head down. She was mumbling, but incoherently. J. J. sat close by watching her intently. Neither could understand anything the prisoner was saying. J. J. stood. Martha glanced up as they approached the cell door and then quickly looked back down. J. J. unlocked the door and walked into the cell. Taking the plate from Sarah, he placed it on the table before picking up the untouched piece of pork fat from the previous night.

"I killed her," Martha said in a monotone. "I killed her." J. J. paused. Maybe he should try to speak with her right now. Sarah, standing just outside the cell door listened intently. J. J. spoke, "Who did you kill, Martha?" Martha looked up at J. J. "She was trying to kill me, so I killed her," she said. "She hit me in the back with something."[50]

J. J. again asked, "Who did you kill, Martha?"

Martha broke down, wailing like a wounded animal. She continued, "They said they were going to kill me! They pulled down the windows and blinds and kept me a long time…my head, it hurts…I got on top of her and I struck her."[51] She was rambling now.

Seizing the opportunity, J. J. asked her if she felt bad about the killing. "No, no… I don't feel bad, so long as I didn't do it to be mean," she explained. When she spoke of the killing, there was a certain gleam in her eye, and a hideous smile.[52] Now her demeanor had changed and she started to become more agitated. J. J. surmised it was due to the morphine he had given her the night before.

J. J. left what would have to pass for breakfast on the table and handed the other plate to Sarah as he left the cell.

Turnkey Landenburger had returned home after his long night in the cold jail guarding prisoners. Harrington, another turnkey, was his replacement. Harrington looked in on Martha right after being given instructions by J. J. He saw the woman seated on the floor and could hear her wailing now. He returned to the first floor of the jail, leaving the prisoner alone in her cell.

Several hours had passed when Harrington began to hear her raving again. As he walked to the second floor, he could see Martha standing near the back corner of her cell smashing her head against the iron slats that made up the walls. She was hitting her head so hard Harrington was certain she would begin to bleed at any moment. He yelled for help and started toward the cell to restrain her. As he turned the tumbler in the lock, Martha stopped what she was doing and turned toward him. She began to sing and then to pray. Harrington stood transfixed, just watching her. After Martha finished her simple melody and benediction, she collapsed on the cell floor in a fit.[53] Harrington quickly entered the cell and, to his relief, there was no blood. He thought to himself that the prisoner would surely have a headache later, as her head would almost certainly be black and blue.

Dr. Sidney Culver in Mason was contacted and came right away to the jail. He was able to assess that the woman's self-inflicted wound wasn't as bad as it appeared. And by that point, Martha had calmed considerably.

J. J. spoke with Doc Culver after he left the cell. He told the physician about the Williamston killing in extensive detail. Culver had recognized Martha. Seven years prior, she had lived in Mason. As he described the situation to J. J., she had come to him and demanded treatment in an incoherent way. For some time, Doc Culver had tried to help her, but it was apparent to him that she should have been placed in the asylum years earlier. Culver had told Martha's brother Richard he should make application through the probate court to have her declared insane. Continuing his dialogue with J. J., Culver said he had actually received a letter from Martha at one point telling him that she was going to Pennsylvania to marry a doctor by the name of Kenyon. She told Culver the Pennsylvania doctor had received her letters, and she was begging him to come take her.[54] There was no doubt in Culver's mind that Martha's letter displayed her insanity.

With that being said, J. J. bid the doctor good day and began to prepare the paperwork that would be needed. Harrington was instructed to keep a constant watch of Martha until the upcoming hearing.

By noontime, Harrington had made several checks of Martha. Each time she was seated back on the cell floor in the same position she had been found early that morning, always with her hands clasped behind her head. On occasion, she would be crying or mumbling.

J. J. had left the jail and headed to the city hall to meet with John Squires, Justice of the Peace for the City of Mason. J. J. had certain protocol in every criminal case he had to follow. It was especially necessary in this case as Martha was already in custody. J. J. would have to file a written Complaint with the justice, and based on that Complaint the justice would give J. J. an arrest warrant directing that the woman be brought before him. The Complaint, under oath and in writing, for the charge of murder was filed with Justice Squires less than 24 hours after the killing. It was Saturday, April 24. The last lines of the Complaint read:

> "...Wherefore the said John J. Rehle, Sheriff prays that said Martha Haney may be apprehended, and held to answer this Complaint, and further dealt with in relation to the same as law and justice may require."[55]

Upon presentation of the Complaint to Justice Squires, the latter wrote out the Criminal Warrant formally charging Martha with the murder of her mother-in-law. The Criminal Warrant, in Justice Squire's handwriting, read:

> "**To the Sheriff or any Constable of said County, Greeting**: **Whereas** John J. Rehle, Sheriff of said County of Ingham hath this day made complaint in writing and on oath, to me John C. Squires, a Justice of the Peace of the City of Mason in said county, that, heretofore, to wit: on the 23rd day of April A. D. 1897 at the Village of Williamston in the county aforesaid, as the said John J. Rehle, Sheriff, is informed and believes, and has good reason to believe, one Martha Haney, late of the Village of Williamston on the said 23rd day of April, A. D 1897, at the said Village of Williamston, in said county of Ingham, aforesaid, feloniously, willfully, and of her malice aforethought, did kill and murder one Maria Haney, **And Whereas**, on examination, on oath, of the said John J. Rehle, Sheriff by me, the said Justice of the Peace that said offense has been committed, and there is just cause to suspect the said Martha Haney to have been guilty thereof; therefore, **IN THE NAME OF THE PEOPLE OF THE STATE OF MICHIGAN**, you, and each of you, are hereby commanded forthwith to arrest the said Martha Haney and bring her before me said Justice of the Peace to be dealt with according to law.
>
> Given under my hand and seal, at the City of Mason in said County on the 24th day of April, A. D. 1897.
>
> John C. Squires Justice of the Peace"[56]

J. J., now having the legal documentation he needed to proceed with the case, would take Martha before Justice Squires on Monday, April 26, to hear the charges presented against her.

It was late in the day when a visitor arrived at the jail to see Martha. It was her brother, Richard Pierce. Richard lived in Mason with his family, and word had spread far beyond where the crime had occurred. He had learned of his sister's incarceration from friends of the family. He met with J. J. at the sheriff's residence after Loranger had left for the train station to return to Williamston. J. J. told Pierce all the details of the gory murder his sister had committed. He recounted Martha's attempt to take her own life by smashing her head against the jail cell wall. Richard said nothing. He only turned his gaze to the floor and slowly moved his head back and forth. Richard already knew of his sister's insanity. For several years he had tried to help her, but he'd been unsuccessful.

He asked if he might be able to see her. They walked slowly to the jail portion of the building, and J. J. accompanied Richard to her cell. Martha was now sleeping, likely as a result of the morphine she had been given earlier. J. J. and Richard spoke softly as they discussed the circumstances of her incarceration. Hearing the men's voices, Martha began to awaken.

She looked up, and, although her gaze fell upon her brother, she looked through him, seemingly unable to recognize him. Richard appeared ashamed of seeing his sister at the point she had reached in her sorry existence.

J. J. asked, "Martha, do you know Dick?" She looked at her brother. "I don't know you. Never saw you before," she replied. Richard spoke up, "Martha, can't you remember me? I'm your brother Dick." Martha's next statement confirmed what Richard already knew; his sister was insane. She said, "No, Jesus has got him. I don't know you." J. J. joined the conversation again by asking Martha, "Who has got old Mariah Haney?" Martha's reply didn't surprise either man: "Jesus, of course." J. J.'s questioning continued as he asked her why she had committed the crime. She replied, "My mother came from heaven and told me to do it." With that, Martha began to pray. She dropped to her knees and tried coaxing J. J. and Richard to kneel as she prayed. When neither man did, she began a new melody:

"O, I can't go to heaven, to hell I must go. Murderers don't go to heaven, and that is where I'm bound to go."[57]

She repeated this melody again and again then stood up in the middle of the cell. Her stance turned rigid just before she fell to the floor in another of her fits.

The sheriff had never seen a person so mentally disturbed. He decided he would take extra care in watching over Martha to ensure she wouldn't try to take her own life again.

As the two men left Martha's cell, J. J. explained that the coroner's inquest had been held in Williamston the pervious afternoon in front of Justice McEnally. He told Richard of the formal arraignment before Justice Squires in Mason that was expected to be on Monday. He asked Richard if he would be able to attend the proceeding. Richard agreed that it might help calm Martha if he were there.

Richard knew this wouldn't be easy. His sister hadn't recognized him, and he could tell she was beyond the point of any help. His thoughts turned to the poor old woman's family in Williamston and what they must be going through. Pierce still struggled to comprehend the macabre crime his sister had committed.

Richard had met his sister's husband Alfy before, but had never really come to know him. He also knew of his sister's children, his own flesh and blood, and how they had been given away for adoption at very young ages. He was thankful for that, not knowing what harm might otherwise have befallen them at the hands of their insane mother.

His emotions could hardly be contained as he left the jail. Richard's only objectives now were to see that his sister received a fair hearing, to support her in this trying time, and to assure that she would never be able to do anything like this to anyone else ever again. Sadly, Richard accepted his sister's guilt. The single tear rolling down his cheek seemed icy cold.

Richard stopped at the jail again on Sunday, but there was still no recognition from Martha. While his heart was broken from seeing his sister in the cold, dark cell, he couldn't help but mourn Mariah's death too. Her funeral had been the previous day - the day after the killing. He didn't attend, but he was sure the entire village of Williamston must have been at the Baptist Church when Mrs. Haney was eulogized and her children grieved.

Richard didn't understand his sister's illness, and she didn't seem to recognize him. Still, he knew it would be his obligation to be there for her. He would attend all of the upcoming court proceedings. The ultimate outcome was certain; he knew deep in his heart where his sister would be spending the rest of her life.

It had been two days since the killing and a week since Easter Sunday. The spring term for the country schools had started two weeks earlier. Summer was fast approaching.

Martha sat in the center of her cell with her head between her legs, still staring at the floor, just as she had done most of the time since her incarceration. The occasional outbursts of wailing became a regular occurrence. She mumbled incoherently on several occasions throughout the day. She ranted so much that no one could understand anything she was trying to say. Martha had eaten very little in the mornings, but she consumed even less at night. The meager slice of pork fat regularly served as nightly fare was consistently left untouched.

THE CIRCUIT COURT

After J. J. filed the Complaint of murder against Martha the day following the murder, he spoke to Probate Judge Porter in an attempt to have Martha simply declared insane, thus ensuring her incarceration at the Michigan Asylum for the Dangerous and Criminally Insane in Ionia. Unfortunately, Judge Porter told him that, given the coroner's inquest and the findings of Justice McEnally, the matter had passed beyond his jurisdiction. Judge Porter told J. J. that even if Martha had been adjudicated insane at some time prior to the killing, a murder was still likely as it would have been impossible to send Martha to the asylum in Kalamazoo due to overcrowded conditions there.[58]

Once the Probate Judge told him he was unable to act, J. J. anticipated the next step in the legal process. It was the March term of the Circuit Court, so after the hearing in Mason before Justice Squires, he would have to accompany the murderess to the Circuit Court in Lansing. There she would either be tried or declared insane and sent to the asylum in Ionia.

Richard also knew what the next step in the judicial process would be. As he left the jail on Saturday, he told J. J. that he would help accompany his sister to the court in Lansing. J. J. also decided to have Sarah come with them on the trip.

On Sunday evening, as J. J. prepared for the arraignment the following day, Martha lay on the floor of her cell sleeping intermittently. Like each of the previous evenings, her meal went untouched.

While Martha was fading in and out of sleep, Richard was at home explaining the court process to his wife Eliza. It had been so very hard for him to hear of the killing, listening to the brutal details of Mariah's death while knowing that his sister was the killer. Richard fought back tears as he tried to describe the murder, being careful not to reveal too much about the graphic nature of the killing to his wife. It didn't matter. Eliza already knew.

It was Monday morning, April 26, when Richard met J. J. and Sarah at the jail. J. J. would be meeting with the justice of the peace.

John Robinson would arrive by train from Williamston and attend the meeting as well. The justice would require written affidavits from both the sheriff and Robinson regarding the vicious murder of the previous Friday and take their testimony under oath.

The sheriff and Pierce went to the second floor of the jail along with Sarah. J. J. told Martha they would be going to her court hearing. She was standing near the cell door waiting for them with the same blank stare she exhibited since she was brought in. She slowly extended her two arms in front of her as J. J. unlocked the cell door. He gently put the shackles around her small wrists and clicked them shut.

The group then walked across the courthouse square to the office of the Justice of the Peace where the arraignment was held.

Justice Squires wrote:

> "The examination of John Robinson and John J. Rehle, Sheriff, taken before me, John C. Squires, a Justice of the Peace of the city of Mason, in the said county, on the 26th day of April, A.D. 1897, in the presence and hearing of Martha Haney, charged before me by John J. Rehle, Sheriff of said County of Ingham, when having upon the 23rd day of April, A. D. 1897, at the Village of Williamston, in the County aforesaid, as the said John J. Rehle, Sheriff, is informed and believes, and has good reason to believe, one Martha Haney, late of the Village of Williamston, on the said 23rd day of April, A. D. 1897, at the said Village of Williamston, in the said County of Ingham aforesaid, feloniously, willfully, and of her malice aforethought, did kill and murder one Maria [sic] Haney, contrary to the form of the statute in such case made and provided, and against the peace and dignity of the People of the State of Michigan."

Martha stood very still, staring blankly at nothing in particular. When the Justice asked her to describe what had occurred, Martha would not speak. The examination continued with the extremely detailed sworn statements of Robinson and the sheriff. Justice Squires concluded the hearing by reading the hand-written statements of both John Robinson and J. J.

At the close of the examination, Justice Squires wrote:

> "To the Circuit Court of the County of Ingham
>
> People of the State of Michigan v Martha Haney: Justice's Return
>
> I, John C. Squires, a Justice of the Peace of the City of Mason, do hereby certify and return to said Circuit Court, that on the 26th day of April, A. D. 1897, Martha Haney was brought before me for examination, touching the offense charged in the annexed Complaint and Warrant of Arrest.
>
> That said Martha Haney after hearing the charge as stated in the Warrant of Arrest distinctly read to her, did not plead thereto, but stood mute; thereupon I, the said Justice of the Peace, proceeded to an examination touching the said offense, and said examination having been had, and witnesses having been produced and sworn before me and in the presence of said Martha Haney, and their testimony taken in writing, and said testimony having been signed by said witnesses in the presence of said respondent, after hearing the same read over to them respectively in the presence and hearing of said respondent-and said examination being had on the 26th day of April, A. D. 1897; and it appearing to me, the said Justice, that said offense charged in said Complaint and Warrant had been committed, that the same is not cognizable by a Justice of the Peace; and after having ascertained and adjudged that there was probable cause to believe the said respondent to be guilty thereof; and I further found that the said respondent, Martha Haney, at the time she committed the said act was an

insane person; thereupon she was by me committed to the common jail of said county to await trial or until otherwise legally discharged.

I further certify and return that the testimony so taken on said examination, and the Complaint and Warrant of Arrest, and all other papers pertaining to said offense, are annexed hereto and herewith returned to said Circuit Court.

Given under my hand, at the City of Mason, in said County, this 26th day of April, A. D., 1897.

John C. Squires, Justice of the Peace"[59]

Thus, at the close of the hearing, Martha Haney was remanded to the custody of J. J. to be held pending proceedings in the Circuit Court.

The following day, Tuesday, April 27, J.J., Richard, Sarah, and the murderess took a carriage from the jail to the Central Michigan railroad depot in Mason to board the train to Lansing. They would be met at the Lansing depot by an officer from the city and escorted to city hall.

The station agent at the depot in Mason had been asked to hold the train until their arrival. As the horse and carriage came to a halt, steam slowly poured from the smoke stack on the engine idling on the tracks. J. J. and Richard both helped Martha step from the carriage and slowly walked her to the first passenger car. Sarah followed close behind. They sat in the first two seats, with J. J. seated next to Martha.

With the shrill of the whistle, the train slowly moved away from the depot heading north toward the Capital City. J. J. occasionally glanced over at Martha, who mumbled sporadically. To Sarah, the 35-minute ride to Lansing seemed an eternity. Even though J. J. and Richard were both there, she feared that Martha might lapse back into an uncontrollable frenzied state.

Lansing had been named the state capital of Michigan in 1847 after it was mandated in the state constitution that the capital be relocated from the city of Detroit. The papers often referred to the Exodus of 1847 when reposting on the large number of people who moved from Mason to Lansing following that event. Still, there were enough businessmen left in Mason to keep the village alive.

The Governor's office was in Detroit, and he only came to Lansing for sessions of the Legislature. One of the legislature's concerns was that Detroit's proximity to the border made the city vulnerable to invasions by British forces in Canada. At the time, there were less than 20 residents in Lansing Township, and the House of Representatives decided on that location for the capitol more out of frustration than anything else, as they couldn't agree on any of the other suitable locations throughout the state that had been suggested. By 1859, Lansing had grown to over 3,000 residents, far more than the number of citizens in the small town of Mason, which remained the Ingham County seat. By 1870, Lansing's population had grown to over 5,000.

Built in 1847, the original capitol building was constructed of wood. By the end of the civil war, the small building could barely accommodate the business of state government. The heating and lighting were limited at best. The building was warmed only by large wood stoves. Until 1861, illumination was strictly by candlelight, and there was no fire protection for the abundance of records being stored there. Lighting was improved in 1872 when the building was piped for gas. Not surprisingly, between 1861 and 1870, every session of the legislature included a discussion about the construction of a new capitol building. When a call went out for architectural designs for a new building, several plans were offered by different contractors. The plans of Elijah Myers from Springfield, Illinois, were finally approved and construction on a grandiose replacement building commenced in 1872.

On January 1, 1879, Michigan's new capitol building in Lansing was dedicated in a grand ceremony. The building was of Palladian-style architecture of Greek and Roman origin. The main part featured a large dome over the center portion, with two separate office wings extending in opposite directions. The dome was 265 feet in height with a diameter of 44 feet, 6 inches.

Many of the lawyers practicing in Ingham County had offices in Lansing because of its rapidly rising population. Many residents in Lansing had cases against the State. It made perfect sense that lawyers should be near their clients. Yet, the County's circuit court remained located in Mason. In every other state, the capital also served as the county seat. In 1850, when Lansing was named as the state's capital, a rivalry developed between the two. At the time, Mason still had a larger population than Lansing.

If a matter were directed to the circuit court, inevitably lawyers from Lansing would have to take a train to the county seat in Mason, thus requiring a return trip to Lansing, and not infrequently an overnight's stay in Mason before that return trip.

Frank Dodge, a young Eaton County attorney who had a practice south of Lansing in the small village of Eaton Rapids, often made trips to Charlotte, Eaton County's seat, for court appearances. He fully understood the hardships of traveling to the courts.

In 1879, Dodge relocated to Lansing. In 1882 he was elected to the Michigan House of Representatives. As part of his new position, he served on several committees, and, in 1883, Dodge introduced a bill that specified at least two of the regular terms of the Ingham County Circuit Court would be held in Lansing, rather than Mason, commencing in that year and continuing in each year thereafter. A second part of the bill specified the only preconditions for this accommodation: the City Council in Lansing would provide a place to hold court and a suitable jail for prisoners to be housed during court sessions. Both the location of the court and the jail were to be inspected and approved by the judge or the prosecuting attorney.

Debate raged between Lansing and Mason over what had come to be known as the "Dodge Bill." While the bill was quickly passed, it incited such a feud that Michigan's Governor Begole agreed to hear both sides of the debate between Lansing and Mason. A former Ingham County Prosecutor, H. P. Henderson argued that the bill was unconstitutional and asked the governor not to sign it into law. He submitted over 3,000 signatures from the out-county area opposing the bill.

On the opposite side of the aisle, Lansing Attorney Martin Montgomery argued for the Dodge Bill to be signed into law. His position was a very practical one: The bill simply allowed people in the northern part of the county to have access to the county court system nearer to their homes. He assured Governor Begole that both the senate and the house had studied the constitutionality of the bill and found it valid. After hearing both sides of the debate, the Governor signed the bill in early May.

Even after the passage of the Dodge Bill, there was continued debate. A letter published in the Republican by Lansing members of the Ingham Bar and others described the costs of conducting business in Mason for years and complained that the current means of transportation didn't allow the lawyers to arrive in Mason until 11:00 a.m. Further, if they intended to return to Lansing on the same day, they would have to leave at 5:00 p.m. before the courts had even adjourned for the day. They explained in their open letter that there would be a decided savings to the people of Ingham County as a whole if the bill remained in effect. On October 4, Justices Thomas R. Sherwood and James R. Campbell issued their opinions after months of appeals and petitions were filed involving the matter. The opinion totaled 18 pages, and in the end, Justice Campbell summarized the opinion by finding the Dodge bill to be valid.

On Monday, October 8, 1883, the first term of circuit court opened in the common council rooms of Lansing's City Hall. It was not until 1891 when the 30th Judicial Circuit Court was established, and it included both Ingham and Livingston County, at which time Governor Winans appointed Judge Rollin H. Person to the vacant judgeship.

The new Lansing City Hall was dedicated on January 4, 1897, just four months before the killing in Williamston. It was the city's first municipally owned building. Bonds had been authorized in 1894 to build the large structure on the southeast corner of Ottawa Street and Capital Avenue. With city administrators still wanting to move the county seat from Mason to Lansing, the building was made large enough to accommodate offices for the Mayor, treasurer, clerk, assessor and the police department. These offices were located in the basement of the building. Upon its completion, the City Hall had electric lights, running water, and indoor bathrooms. Because of the desire to move the county seat, it also included accommodations for the Ingham County Circuit Court and the Ingham County Probate Court.

Constructed of large, grey brick, the City Hall stood four stories tall. The new building was known for its large, four-sided clock tower with a steep, angled roof that stood over the main entrance. The clock tower struck on Standard Time instead of Sun Time, which would vary by 20 to 25 minutes. Large brick arches over the entrances greeted visitors to the grand building. Inside, a modern electric elevator could be used instead of the stairways.

When Martha arrived with her escorts she attracted considerable attention. As the foursome walked through the lobby toward the elevator, Martha was a pitiful sight and still mumbled incoherently.

The gate across the elevator opened to allow them access. Martha was extremely apprehensive about stepping in, having never seen such a contraption. Finally J. J. and Richard were able to convince her the elevator was safe and she warily entered the small space. The gate closed behind the four occupants. The cubicle was very small and moved ever so slowly. Nevertheless it steadily transported them to the third floor.

At 11:00 a.m., the Circuit Court was called to order and Martha stood before the Honorable Judge Rollin H. Person for her arraignment. A portrait of John Marshall, Chief Justice of the United States Supreme Court, adorned the wall behind Judge Person's desk, with Michigan Supreme Court Justices Tomas M. Cooley and James V. Campbell on either side of the Chief Justice.

Judge Person, with his high forehead, gray, receding hairline and neatly trimmed gray beard looked distinguished as he sat behind the desk in his long, black robe. He was every bit a gentlemen.

Born in Livingston County, Judge Person had attended Howell High School and, at an early age, had already decided on his future occupation as a lawyer. Even before attending law school, he had started reading law textbooks under the direction of another Howell attorney, Daniel Shields. His self-study prior to law school was accepted as the equivalent of one year at one of the finer schools in the country. He graduated from the University of Michigan Law School in 1872 and was admitted to the bar the following year.

After his education as a lawyer was complete, Person relocated to Nebraska where he began his private practice. Two years later, crop devastation hit that state and he found it hard to collect the monies his clients owed to him. He decided to return to Michigan.

Person served as the Circuit Court Commissioner in Livingston County in 1877 and was appointed as a judge of the 30th Circuit Court in 1890. The following year he was chosen as the Chief Judge of the Circuit. Livingston County was a part of the 30th Circuit at the time.

Rollin Person was known as a leader in the Livingston bar even prior to his appointment to the bench. His knowledge of the law, judicial temperament, ability to grasp points made by other attorneys, quick discerning of pertinent evidence and ready decision-making, separated him from many of the other judges throughout the state.

The Honorable Rollin Person, Used with Permission of the Michigan Supreme Court Historical Society

Presenting the Martha Haney case for the People of the State of Michigan was Ingham County Prosecuting Attorney Alva Cummins. This 28-year-old democrat had been born on a farm near the village of Perry, northeast of Lansing in 1869. When he was twelve years old, his family moved to the Dakota Territory and took up wheat farming. While there, Cummins studied at Groton College in South Dakota and later moved back to Michigan studying at Kalamazoo College. The total time he spent at these colleges amounted to five years. The reputation he developed in college of thorough scholarship and attention to detail preceded him. He studied under Lansing attorney Sam Kilbourne, the man who organizd the first Ingham County

Bar Association. Kilbourne was married to the daughter of Ingham County's first lawyer, John W. Burhcard. Cummins, who Kilbourne considered one of his best students, once complimented his mentor by saying he, "Had one of the keenest legal minds...No one could go into a suit with Sam Kilbourne without knowing a real legal battle was on." Cummins, after having studied under Kilbourne, was well suited for the position of Prosecuting Attorney. Opening his own practice in Mason on August 1, 1891, it was said that Cummins combined the three qualities that every good lawyer should have, those being natural ability, education, and experience.

Ingham County Prosecuting Attorney Alva M. Cummins (source www.ancestry.com)

As Martha Haney stood in the open courtroom, Judge Person took his seat, reviewing the paperwork presented by the Prosecuting

Attorney Cummins. It read:

> "...The Circuit Court for the County of Ingham. Of the March term to [sic] therefore in the year, 1897.
>
> Ingham County, ss.
>
> A. M. Cummins, prosecuting attorney in and for the county of Ingham for and in behalf of the People of the State of Michigan, comes into said court in the March term thereof in the year 1897, and give the court here to understand and be informed, that heretofore, to wit: on the twenty third day of April, 1897, at the village of Williamston in the county of Ingham, one Martha Haney, late of said village of Williamston, feloniously, willfully and of her malice aforethought one Maria Haney [sic] did kill and murder contrary to the form of the statute in such case made and provided and against the peace and dignity of the People of the State of Michigan.
>
> A.M. Cummins
>
> Prosecuting Attorney."[60]

After reviewing the document provided by Prosecutor Cummins, Judge Person looked up at the woman standing directly in front of him. After asking her name and receiving no response, he turned to the prosecuting attorney and asked if the woman standing before him was Martha Haney. Cummins answered yes. The judge's gaze returned to the woman, telling her that she was being charged with murder and asking her if she understood. Her response was rambling and incoherent. Judge Person could understand only part of what she said. She acknowledged she had killed the old woman, but said she had to do it. Judge Person studied her face as she mumbled and looked around the room. Then she looked directly at the Judge and stated, "There are some things I won't tell you, even if I'm killed for it."[61]

Judge Person took a deep breath, making some notes as he exhaled. As he finished, he instructed his court clerk to enter a "not guilty" plea for Martha.

Richard Pierce sat in the back row trying to keep a low profile. He could only look toward the floor, his right hand covering his mouth as once again, tears welled in his eyes. He sat alone, as he had insisted his wife Eliza not attend the proceedings. It would be too much for her to handle.

Martha stared into blank space, occasionally breaking down and beginning to wail. She would occasionally mumble, but no one could understand anything she might be saying.

It became very clear to Judge Person that the woman standing before him, accused of murdering her mother-in-law, was not in her right mind. There were court procedures that he would have to follow, even though he knew what the final outcome would be.

Judge Person asked J. J. if Martha had any family members present. Richard raised his hand ever so slightly. After determining the relationship between Martha and Richard, the Judge asked if Richard would be able to afford representation for his sister. Sadly, Richard had never thought about a lawyer for Martha. He knew she didn't have any money, and he couldn't afford to pay one for her. Judge Person, having known the answer before Richard had given it, appointed Lansing attorney Charles F. Hammond to represent Martha.

Charles Hammond, whose offices occupied three rooms in Lansing's Hollister Building, lived on North Washington Street. Hammond was acquainted with both Judge Person and Alva Cummins personally. At forty years old, he had formed a local law practice with Jay P. Lee, another local attorney. His sparse, gray hair, balding head and round spectacles made him easily identifiable in the legal community. Hammond was well known among his colleagues. He had himself served as the Ingham County Prosecuting Attorney from 1887 to 1888. Having spent his formidable years in Mason as a child,

Hammond attended the University of Michigan for one year, then returned to Mason and was admitted to the bar in 1878. The following year, he opened his own practice with J. P. Lee, Harry Silsbee, and former Supreme Court Justice Harry Hooker.

Charles F. Hammond, Martha Haney's Defense Attorney
(source www.ancestry.com)

Judge Person was aware that before he could proceed any further in this matter he would have to appoint a commission to determine if Martha Haney was insane.

If Martha was tried on the charge of murder and found not guilty by reason of her insanity, she would be acquitted of the murder, at which point he would send her to asylum, and, if she was eventually determined to have regained her sanity, she would be released.

Judge Person had several thoughts going through his mind. He recalled the Herre case, just as J. J. had. He knew that if he appointed a commission to determine Martha's sanity prior to trial, and if she were determined to be insane, he would send her to the asylum. Then, in the event she recovered, the murder charge could still be brought against her after her release from the institution. The defendant in the Herre case was tried and acquitted by reason of insanity before she was sent to the asylum, and because she had been acquitted, she couldn't be re-tried for the murder of her son upon her release.

Judge Person knew he had no choice. Fully expecting to send her to the Ionia asylum following their examination, he appointed a commission of three doctors to determine the sanity of Martha Haney. This case was clearly different than the Herre case. Like J. J. and Cummins, there was no doubt in Judge Person's mind that Martha Haney was insane, even before hearing the findings of any commission. Moreover, he doubted if she could ever be cured.

The judge asked Prosecutor Cummins if any doctors had attended to Martha while she had been in custody or when she had previously lived in Mason. Cummins had done his homework. He reported that Martha had once sought the assistance of Dr. Sidney Culver when she lived in Mason. Hearing that, Judge Person appointed Dr. Culver, along with Drs. Alexander McMillan and E. D. North of Lansing, to pass upon her state of mind.

Dr. Sidney Culver was a prominent physician and surgeon in Mason. He had graduated from the University of Michigan Medical School where he had served as his Senior Class Historian. After commencement, he immediately settled in Mason. Born in 1856, his father, Captain John C. Culver, was a veteran of the civil war. He had one half-brother, Elias, who was a jeweler in Mason. Dr. Culver's first wife had died when she was washing windows at his Jefferson Street office and fell, suffering a fractured skull. He remarried after her death. Active in the small community where he had established his practice, he had been First Chancellor Commander of the Mason Knights of Pythias Lodge and had also been a part of the Masonic Order.

A descendant of Scottish Highlanders, Dr. Alexander McMillan had been a prominent physician in the city of Lansing for many years and enjoyed a reputation for having the utmost integrity. He was born in the County of Glengarry, Canada in 1845. His father was a farmer who had settled in Canada in 1798. McMillan lived for some time in Chicago where he was in the mercantile business, but he lost his store in the great Chicago fire of 1871. He then moved to New York City and began his medical training at the Belleview Hospital Medical College. After a year there, he moved to the Long Island Hospital Medical College where he completed his education and graduated in 1874. Dr. McMillan had always been attracted to Michigan, and after settling in Lansing he became a member of the Lansing Medical Society, even serving as its president. Dr. McMillan's older brother was also a physician in Ontario.

Born in 1841, Doctor Elmer D. North had served in the civil war for four years. He had attended Albion College after the War of the Rebellion, graduating in 1870. Following his graduation from Albion, he became a schoolteacher prior to practicing medicine and served as Superintendent of the Ingham County Schools. In 1882, he attended the Detroit Medical College for two years. Upon completing his education there, he opened his practice as a physician in Lansing. Dr. North had never married. When it came to his skills as a physician, his colleagues described him as having a "very marked ability."

Now the decision of Martha's sanity rested with the three doctors making up the commission. Judge Person knew they would have several things to consider before arriving at a conclusion. Their determination would be based on common law principles handed down from the United Kingdom and accepted in this country in the mid-1800s. These principles were applied to determine an accused person's mental state at the time a crime was committed.

On January 20, 1843, in the parish of St. Martin in the Fields, England, Daniel M'Naghten, a Scottish woodcutter, shot Edward Drummond, the secretary for Sir Robert Peel, in the back. Drummond managed to survive until April 25, 1843, when he died. At the time of the shooting, M'Naghten thought Drummond was in fact, Peel. His motive behind the murder was his belief that Peel was responsible for his personal and financial failures and that he was being persecuted by the Tory party. Nine people testified that M'Naghten was insane, thus leading to his acquittal on the murder charge due to his insanity.

Queen Victoria and a great many of the British public were outraged by the jury's verdict. The Queen asked the House of Lords to conduct a review of the verdict. A panel of judges was asked to address five issues put forth in the form of questions regarding a person's sanity and legal procedures to be employed in the course of a person's trial.

The first issue, in part, sought a clarification of the law *"respecting alleged crimes committed by a person afflicted with insane delusion."* The judge's response was straightforward and ultimately set the standard for the insanity defense in the United States:

> *"To render a person irresponsible for crime on account of unsoundness of mind, the unsoundness should, according to the law as it has long been understood and held, be such as rendered him incapable of knowing right from wrong."*-

The second issue addressed proper questions proposed to a jury: *What are the proper questions to be submitted to the jury...when a person alleged to be afflicted with insane delusion respecting one or more particular subjects or persons, is charged with the commission of a crime, and insanity is set up as a defence [sic]?* The response was as follows:

> "The questions necessarily to be submitted to the jury, are those questions of fact, which are raised on the record….In performing his duty, it is sometimes necessary or convenient [for the judge] to inform the jury as to the law; and if, on a trial such as is suggested in the question, he should have occasion to state what kind an degree of insanity would amount to a defence [sic], it should be stated conformable to what I have mentioned in my answers to the first question"-

The third question the judges were asked to opine on read: *In what terms ought the questions to be left to the jury, as to the prisoner's state of mind at the time when the act was committed?*

Terms used to assist the jury in their findings was the crux of the response to this third question:

> "There are no terms which the Judge is by law required to use. They should not be inconsistent with the law as above stated, but should be such as, in the discretion of the Judge, are proper to assist the jury in coming to a right conclusion as to the guilt of the accused."-

Moving to the fourth issue, the essential question presented was whether or not insanity would excuse a defendant from his responsibility for the commission of a crime. It read…*If a person under an insane delusion, as to existing facts, commits an offence [sic] in consequence thereof, is he thereby excused?*

In essence, they judges again referred the House of Lords back to their response to the first question. They said that a determination would have to be made with regard to whether the defendant's state of mind, "…rendered him incapable of knowing right from wrong."-

The final question to the judges posited the issue of whether a diagnosis could be made by a medical doctor if the doctor had never previously seen the defendant, but had been present at the trial: *Can a medical man conversant with the disease of insanity, who never saw the prisoner previously at the trial, but who was present during the whole trial and the examination of all the witnesses, be asked his opinion as to the state of the prisoner's mind at the time of the doing the act?*

The response:

> "The medical man, under the circumstances supposed, cannot in strictness be asked his opinion in the terms above stated, because each of those questions involves the determination of the truth of the faces deposed to, which it is for the jury to decide, and the questions are not mere questions upon a matter of science, in which case such evidence is admissible. But where the facts are admitted or not disputed, and the question becomes substantially one of science only, it may be convenient to allow the question to be put in that general form, though the same cannot be insisted on as a matter of right."-

With that, on June 19, 1843, the judges reversed the jury verdict in the M'Naghten case.[62] By their responses to these inquiries, the measuring stick for anyone attempting to rely upon an insanity defense was established. Having come to be known as the M'Naghten Rule, it was quickly embraced by the American courts and legislature and would become the standard by which an accused's mental capacity would be determined for the next 150 years.

If the Commission appointed by Judge Person came to the conclusion that, because of her mental condition, Martha didn't know that killing Mariah was wrong, then she would be declared legally insane.

It would take some time to notify the physicians of their

appointment to this commission. The court clerk was instructed to contact each of the doctors immediately.

Judge Person ordered a recess until the early afternoon, hoping that the doctors would have received notification by then and could start their inquiry that very day.

J. J., Martha, Richard, and Sarah left the courtroom and walked to the Lansing City Jail where Martha was to be confined until the recess ended. While there, Ruth Shank, an artist used by the local paper, came in and sketched a rendering of Martha.

Martha, while clearly not in her right mind, had enough wits to know that she was in serious trouble. She had been in jail for the past several days. She had stood before judges and she was still in jail. Now they were going to have doctors testify about her sanity. Already leery, she became even more afraid, and, when anyone came near her, she became more frightened. She constantly begged both J. J. and Sarah not to let anyone hurt her. Her whining and plaintive tone was evident now whenever she spoke.

J. J. and Martha, along with Richard, waited patiently for the doctors to arrive. The physicians would speak to all three. After queries, they would collectively give an expert medical opinion as to Martha's sanity both at the time of the murder and afterward.

By mid-afternoon, two of the doctors appointed to the commission had arrived at Lansing City Hall and began to interview J. J. regarding the murder. They asked about the apprehension of the killer, and her actions at the jail in Mason while in custody.

After speaking with J. J., they spoke with Sarah, asking about Martha's demeanor as an inmate the Ingham County Jail. Sarah spoke of Martha's refusal to eat and her attempt at taking her own life by smashing her head against the iron slats that made up her cell. She also told of Martha's ramblings and of her being unable to recognize her own brother.

Richard spoke next with the doctors about Martha's life, where her children might be and what type of childhood she had experienced. It wasn't easy for Richard to describe the life he had watched his younger sister endure, but he knew it was important the doctors knew everything. If Martha were to ever get any help, they would have to have a complete understanding.

Finally, the three medical professionals would speak to the killer herself. Doc Culver had not arrived as yet, so the two other doctors proceeded to the cell without him.

Doc McMillan greeted Martha and tried to begin a dialogue. Martha's mumbling stopped, and her gaze shifted to the floor of the cell. She was silent. After a pause, Doc North decided to try. He asked Martha if she knew where she was or why she was there. Martha's gaze moved from one corner of the cell to the other. A look of sheer terror came over her face. She began to speak to no one in particular. A sudden diatribe was unleashed but it wasn't directed at the doctors. She turned her back on them as she lashed out at someone, or something, unseen.

Not to be discouraged, both doctors moved around to the back side of the cell so they were facing Martha. Doc North tried again. Martha began to wail uncontrollably. Several minutes passed as the doctors waited patiently. She suddenly stopped crying, staring at both of them. "I won't tell you, even if you kill me," as she snarled at both of the doctors.

Doc McMillan tried once more but to no avail. Martha's eyes darted to a corner of the cell and, again, she yelled at no one. She looked back at the two doctors, begging them not to hurt her. She broke down sobbing. It was obvious they wouldn't be able to speak intelligently with her. As the doctors left the cell they glanced at each other but said nothing.

Dr. Culver arrived from Mason late in the day. He was surprised when he learned he had been appointed to the commission assigned to evaluate Martha's mental capacity. Nevertheless, having dealt with her in the past and knowing her state of mind, he knew he was a logical choice.

Dr. Culver spoke with the two Lansing doctors and offered his assessment of Martha's stability based on his encounters with her a few years prior. They, in turn, shared their findings with him. Together, there was no doubt in the physicians' minds, and since they weren't able to converse with Martha, they would have to rely on their interviews with J. J., Sarah, and Richard.

Having completed their assessment, Culver, McMillan and North would offer their expert opinions to the Court. Everyone knew where Martha would likely be spending the rest of her life.

Because of the time, the doctors would have to prepare their opinion during the evening hours and present it to the Court on the morning of Wednesday, April 28.

The court session the following morning would start early, and J. J. had no doubt he and Sarah would be leaving immediately from the court to take Martha to Ionia. She was left in the custody of the Lansing police at the jail for the night as J. J. and Sarah made plans to stay in a downtown hotel for the evening.

Richard felt it was better if he left and headed back to his family in Mason. He was devastated. The train ride back to Mason was agonizingly slow. As he left his sister in the custody of the sheriff, she still had no idea who he was. Richard knew it would likely be the last time he would ever see his sister.

It was shortly after 8:00 am on Wednesday, April 28, when the Ingham County Circuit Court reconvened. The sun glistened through the windows of the courtroom as the magistrate entered. After calling the court to order, Judge Rollin H. Person was handed the opinion of the commission appointed to set the course of Martha Haney's future.

The three doctors were sworn in by the bailiff and asked to present their opinions. Martha, the picture of misery, was led back into the courtroom by J. J.

The commission appointed to assess the sanity of Martha Haney presented the following:

> "We, the undersigned, appointed by the said court to examin [sic] said Martha Haney and to inquire into the facts of her case an [sic] to report the same to the court, do hereby report to said court that in compliance with said appointment we have carefully examined said Martha Haney and have inquired into the facts of her case and do find that she is at this time insane and without sufficient mental capacity to undertake her defense in this case and that she has dangerous and criminal tendencies and is wholly irresponsible for her acts. We base our findings on the following history and mental condition. She has always been considered simple and feeble minded even as a child. She has been subject to epileptic seizures since she was ten years of age. Her mental condition as evidenced by present impairment of mind has evidentially resulted from this epilepsy. She frequently engages in prayer and the singing of devotional songs at inopportune times and places. She presents the appearance of a simple minded person. Her face lacks expression; her conversation is disconnected; she seems to be almost wholly deprived of memory but this loss of memory is partially assumed without any apparent reason. While she sometimes admits the act of killing Maria Haney she does not seem to have any conception of the enormity of the crime or even that she has committed a crime.
>
> *In witness thereof we affixed our hands this 28th day of April, 1897.*
>
> > E. D. North
> >
> > Alexander McMillan
> >
> > Sidney H. Culver"[63]

The judge looked at Hammond, Martha's lawyer, and asked him if he had anything to add. There was no expression on Hammond's face. He could offer nothing and could only concur with the experts. The judge glanced at Martha. She was mumbling incoherently again, and he couldn't understand anything she was saying. He glanced at J. J., and J. J. simply looked back at the judge, much like Mr. Hammond had....expressionless.

Judge Person knew this procedure well. Based on the commission's opinion that Martha Haney was insane, he had no choice. He looked at Hammond. Addressing him, he told Hammond that he, too, agreed with the doctors' collective opinion that Martha Haney was insane at the time of the killing, and, thus, she should be confined to the Asylum for the Dangerous and Criminally Insane in Ionia. The law was very clear regarding the insane. Under Michigan's law, it read:

> "When any person held in prison on a charge of having committed an indictable offense, shall not be indicted by the grand jury by reason of insanity, such jury shall certify that fact to the court; and thereupon, if the discharge or going at large of such insane person shall be deemed manifestly dangerous to the peace and safety of the community, the court may order him [sic] to be retained in prison until the further order of the court, otherwise he [sic] shall be discharged."[64]

Hammond had been watching Martha out of the corner of his eye. As Judge Person completed his statement, he refocused his attention toward the bench and acknowledged Judge Person's ruling.

J. J. stepped over toward Martha and reached for the shackles in his pocket. They were placed once again on Martha's small wrists. J. J., Sarah, and Martha all left the courtroom as she began humming to herself.

They walked back to the elevator and were taken back to the Lansing Police office in the basement. It was barely 9:00 am. At that point, and they were accompanied by a Lansing police officer to one of the three Lansing train depots. J. J. and Sarah would depart Lansing with the convicted killer and accompany her to the Michigan Asylum for the Dangerous and Criminally Insane.

THE ASYLUM

Several definitions of insanity were developing in the 19th century as more asylums were built throughout the country. Social attitudes toward those who suffered from mental disorders in large part influenced the types of care patients were given. Poverty was one of the primary factors many believed caused mental illness. A part of that belief was that with a large increase in population came a proportionate increase in poverty. Thus, it was not surprising that more people were afflicted with mental illness. One of the men who advanced the theoretical relationship between poverty and mental illness was Frederick Engels. In 1869 Engels was referring to the poor when he wrote:

> "They are exposed to the most exciting changes in mental conditions, the most violent vibrations between hope and fear: they are hunted like game, and not permitted to attain piece of mind and quiet enjoyment of life. They are deprived of all enjoyment of life. They are deprived of all enjoyments except that of sexual indulgence and drunkenness and are worked every day to the point of complete exhaustion of their mental and physical energies, and are thus constantly spurred on to the maddest excess in the only two enjoyments at their disposal."[65]

While poverty was considered one cause of mental illness, genetics was also believed to be a contributing factor. The Inheritance Theory held that insanity could be transmitted from generation to generation.

Still another theory, moral degeneracy, declared that the sufferings of some (a certain percentage) of the poor and physically infirm was due to badness of character. Those labeled as lunatics were considered to be most un-reformable. In fact, one researcher noted, "There is nothing that the nation can do for them except to let them die out by leaving them alone." (White, 1885)

From the inheritance and moral degeneracy ideology, eugenics developed. The eugenics theory held that:

> "If a genetically and morally inferior section of society was allowed to propagate freely, it would within a short space of time outnumber the rest of society. Allowing such poor quality individuals to reproduce would reverse the course of evolution, returning human civilization to an animal state."[66]

This theory eventually led to the sterilization of many suffering from mental illness throughout the country.

In 1897, Michigan was the first state in the nation to propose eugenics-based legislation. The bill called for the castration of certain types of criminals and degenerates. Supported by Dr. John Kellogg, the Battle Creek inventor of Corn Flakes who ran a sanitarium himself, the bill never passed. It took another 16 years before Michigan adopted a forced sterilization policy applicable to the mentally defective or insane in public institutions.[67]

In addition to being a victim of poverty and despair, Martha Haney's mental condition may have been rooted in a variety of causes. The source, however, made little difference. While many recognized her insanity prior to the killing, it had neither been officially diagnosed nor treated until it was too late, and her mother-in-law was dead.

It had warmed substantially over the previous several days. After the spring rains, it felt as if summer might be just around the corner. Warm sunshine had replaced cool, cloudy days.

J. J. squinted in the morning sun as he stepped from the carriage with the killer. Given the morning warmth, he thought this would be a perfect day for a train ride, save for having to take an insane murderess to the asylum in Ionia. Sarah, stepping from the carriage after

Martha, prayed silently that the killer wouldn't make a disturbance along the way.

Martha prayed too, quietly to herself, mumbling again as the trio walked toward the waiting train. J. J. was cautious as he watched Martha make her way up the steps of the passenger car. He stood ready should his charge lapse into another violent episode.

This trip would be something new for the sheriff and his wife. While they had been to Ionia on a few occasions by train, they had never been to the asylum. Novelty aside, neither of them was looking forward to this journey.

Anyone in Michigan needing mental health care prior to 1855 could expect to be sent to institutions along the east coast. Brattleboro, Vermont, and Utica, New York, both hosted such facilities. But in that same year, the Sisters at St. Mary's in Detroit began a privately funded effort to treat the mentally ill. In addition to this endeavor, they opened the Michigan State Retreat in 1860, which was a separate facility.

State-funded institutions in Michigan, such as Kalamazoo's Michigan Asylum for the Insane, opened in 1859. Other institutions followed. In 1878, the Eastern Michigan Asylum opened in Pontiac, followed by the Northern Michigan Asylum in 1885. What would later become Martha's new residence in Ionia opened that same year.

In the mid-1800s, moral treatment had come to the forefront of mental health care around the United States. This form of treatment was based on psychosocial and moral discipline. In theory, moral care focused on social welfare and the individual rights of the patients. Shackles and inhumane treatment were to be avoided.

Dr. Benjamin Rush, a Pennsylvania physician whose practice was strictly limited to mental health, was a leader in the development of humane approaches to treating mental illness. He hired staff that would talk to patients, read to them and take them for walks. Unfortunately, he also still exposed patients to bloodletting, purging, hot and cold showers, mercury, tranquilizer chairs, and spinning boards. And for the more severe and violent patients, restraints were not uncommon.

By the late 1800s, in large part, due to of overcrowding and the inability to provide more individualized attention, some asylums were often reduced to nothing more than human zoos, where the wealthy could pay a fee to observe the patients.

Michigan's Asylum for the Dangerous and Criminally Insane was under the direct supervision of Dr. Oscar Russell Long and Dr. W. F. Maxwell.

Dr. Long, born in 1850 in Pennsylvania, spent his first years of regular school in Williamsport, Pennsylvania and the Dickerson Seminary. In 1871 he entered the University of Michigan. The University's medical school had both an orthodox and a homeopathy department. Long chose the Homeopathy Department, and, in 1873, he graduated from the Detroit Homeopathic Hospital.

Homeopathy was first introduced by a German physician, Samuel Hahnemann, in the mid-1800s. Hahnemann believed, through his own trial and error, that the "Law of Similars" allowed a homeopathic doctor to correct symptoms of ill-health with substances that produce similar symptoms in healthy people. The "Law of Similars" had been used by ancient civilizations for hundreds of years, but it was Hahnemann who reduced it to a systematic medical science. Hahnemann's approach to Homeopathy practice included prescribing only one medicine at a time to a patient, and only in very limited doses.

In contrast, orthodox physicians were trained in allopathic, or mainstream medicine, which, in essence, prescribed medications that were opposite of the symptoms in a patient.

Homeopathy continued to grow in popularity over the years

partly because orthodox medicine was ineffective and even dangerous in the 1800s.

In 1874, Dr. Long moved to Ionia and established his general practice. By the time the asylum was completed, the Board of Control appointed him as Superintendent. The Board noted that, with his knowledge and temperament in the study of mental disease, Long was more than qualified to manage the Ionia asylum. In 1881, he was elected President of the Homeopathic Society of Michigan. Later, in 1898, he received an honorary Doctor of Medicine degree from the University of Michigan.

It was well known that the Ionia asylum couldn't be considered a true medical institution since it strictly housed criminals and was not for the public at large. And while there was no provision for homeopathic treatment, Dr. Long practiced it anyway. The treatment at the asylum under his tutelage would always be homeopathic.

Organized under the name of the Michigan Asylum for Dangerous Criminals, the name of the institution, which Dr. Oscar Long's name would become synonymous with, was changed in 1891; it became the Michigan Asylum for the Dangerous and Criminally Insane under Michigan's Public Act 181.

Appropriations by the Michigan Legislature financed the purchase of a large farm to be used for the construction of the institution. The entire complex, which originally included eight buildings and totaled 217 acres, was erected at a cost of over $83,000. Additional appropriations were made in 1891 and in 1895 to increase resident capacity.

On September 7, 1885, the first residents were brought to the asylum. By the end of its first year of operation there were 63 residents. When Martha was dispatched to the asylum in 1897 it housed over 1,000 inmates.

The elegant buildings stood in stark contrast to the residents within. The asylum held convicted, albeit insane, criminals transferred from penal institutions throughout the entire state. Included were insane inmates that were charged, but had been acquitted by reason of insanity, and others, like young Martha Haney, who were sent to the institution directly from the courts without ever having gone through a trial.

It was amazing to Ingham County's sheriff that the asylum was touted as the most successful in all of the country. After all, it could hardly be disputed that insane criminals were the most undesirable people in society. As J. J. realized that the asylum was very successful, so too, did others. It was unlikely that there was another asylum anywhere in the United States that was run as efficiently as the one in Ionia.

The train pulled away from the Lansing depot ever so slowly as steam flowed heavily from the smokestack. The huge iron horse gradually gained momentum as it headed north from the state's Capital City. Martha quietly mumbled to herself. The sheriff and his wife kept a constant watch over her.

As the train made its way through the countryside, it became apparent that the warm, spring day had worked a complete change on nature since the day of the killing. Spring flowers were beginning to sprout from their winter slumber. J. J., still keeping a wary eye on his prisoner, peered out the window of the passenger car. Occasionally he spotted a white-tailed deer standing in a nearby field. J. J. thought to himself that he hadn't seen a more perfect day in a very long time. On the other hand, Sarah wasn't able to enjoy their journey to Ionia. She would be much relieved when their delivery to the asylum was over. On the return trip later in the day, it would just be her and J. J.

The caravan of steam engine, coal tender and passenger cars traveled westward, crossing briefly into Clinton County to the north and continuing into Ionia County to the west. Neither J. J. nor Sarah knew what to expect when they finally arrived at their destination.

After the train entered Ionia County, Martha began to shout. She screamed that her mother had told her to kill the old woman. She screamed so loud that J. J. was certain the engineer could hear her over the deep growl of the steam engine. Trying to calm her, he and Sarah talked hurriedly to the woman. Even when the shouting subsided, Martha's breathing was still heavy and sweat rolled from her forehead.

J. J. knew Martha would never leave the asylum in Ionia. She would be there for the rest of her life. Mercifully the gentle rocking back and forth of the passenger car seemed to have a calming effect on her and she closed her eyes. J. J. wasn't about to let his guard down, but his tension eased slightly.

As Sarah stared out at the passing countryside, J. J. wondered what it must be like to live in a lunatic asylum. Years before, he had read a news article from a New York paper about an asylum in that state. An investigative reporter had written an article exposing the conditions within that asylum. Not able to recall the name of the writer, he could still clearly remember the article's content and the horrid conditions that he'd read about. He hoped better things awaited Martha as the train carrying her to the asylum made its way west.

Nellie Bly was the pen name for American journalist Elizabeth Jane Cochran. Born in 1864, much of Cochran's early work in journalism focused on the plight of working women. After a six-month assignment as an investigative journalist in Mexico, during which she was threatened with incarceration because of her reporting, she returned to the United States. Not surprisingly, she did not hesitate to denounce Mexican dictator Porfirio Diaz.

In 1887, having worked for the *Pittsburgh Dispatch*, she left for New York City and talked her way into a job with Joseph Pulitzer's newspaper The *New York World*. She immediately took an undercover assignment that would lead to reforms within asylums throughout the United States. Cochran agreed to pretend she suffered from insanity in an effort to be admitted to the Women's Lunatic Asylum on Blackwell's Island so she could report on conditions there.

She feigned her insanity so well, thanks to practicing in front of a mirror, that she was admitted to the institution. For ten days she suffered under the harshest of conditions, taking note of the abhorrent way women confined to the asylum were treated.

Cochran's description of the asylum's buildings sounded much like Ionia: Large, stately looking structures surrounded by rolling hills and plush green grass. She described long, bare rooms with large, barred windows. There were benches described as being perfectly straight that were built to hold five people, but often were called upon to seat six. Everything in the main room was spotlessly clean.

She described the food as being scant and barely edible, consisting mostly of tea, thick- cut stale bread and prunes. The women were occasionally fed oatmeal or some cut of what was purported to be beef.

Baths were given only once a week, and each woman was washed in the same water as the others. The same towel was used to dry them all. They wore the same clothing for as long as a month before it was washed.

Cochran reported that each door had to be manually locked and unlocked, and in the event of a fire the inmates were sure to burn to death.

Patients were made to sit from 6:00 a.m. to 8:00 p.m. on the hard, wooden benches without moving, and if they moved they were beaten. They were constantly taunted by the nurses who were supposed to be caring for them.

Exercise consisted of an occasional walk, and the reporter wrote of seeing what she characterized as a "rope line" of women inmates.

She reported they had, "Vacant eyes and meaningless faces, and their tongues uttered meaningless nonsense. One crowd passed and I noted by nose, as well as eyes, that they were fearfully dirty....They were considered the most violent on the island."[68]

Violence within that New York asylum was cruel, to say the least. Cochran described repeated beatings and choking of the inmates by the nursing staff, so much so that the residents were eventually worn down. In describing the beating of one woman, her expose' stated:

> "She grew more hysterical every moment until they pounced upon her and slapped her face and knocked her head in a lively fashion. This made the poor creature cry the more, and so they choked her. Yes, they actually choked her. Then they dragged her out to the closet, and I heard her terrified cries hush into smothered ones. After sever hours absence she returned to the sitting-room, and I plainly saw the marks of their fingers on her throat for the entire day."[69]

Yes, after Martha had been declared insane by the Commission in the Circuit Court of Ingham County, knowing what "Nellie Bly" had reported years earlier, J. J. couldn't help but be concerned about what Martha might face at the asylum in Ionia.

The steam engine chugged to a slow stop at the Ionia depot. The spring warmth overtook J. J. and, for an instant, inhaling the smell of spring, he forgot about his day's task. Then he stepped from the passenger car with his prisoner. Sarah followed a few steps behind.

Martha was tired and weary as they walked toward a waiting carriage that would take them to the west, out of town and to the asylum. J. J. had made sure that Martha had been given morphine before the long journey. The drug seemed to have calmed her. At last she had been able to manage the train ride.

Arrangements had been with the asylum ahead of time. The attendant meeting them with the carriage would ferry them to Martha's final destination.

The dust trail rising from the wheels on the road swirled and formed a cloud behind them as they made their way south away from the small hamlet. Crossing over the Grand River, it was only a short distance before their carriage turned toward the west along the South River Road. The asylum was less than a mile away. As the carriage moved steadily along the south side of the river, J. J. could feel the tension mounting again. He kept a close eye on Martha as the entrance leading to her new home came into view.

Large brick columns marked each side of the private road leading to the asylum. Next to each column was a smaller column with a low brick wall running parallel to the roadway in both directions. The high brick columns gave a stately appearance to the institution that held some of society's most feared.

The entrance ran southwesterly from South River Road and was lined with trees. New spring growth had begun to appear as the carriage passed under overhanging limbs. Cutting between steep hills on either side of the entrance, the carriage followed a slight grade upward. As the carriage reached the top of the hill, the buildings that had been visible from the roadway appeared much larger now. The asylum was nothing like J. J. had imagined it to be.

Set upon a hill, the Michigan Asylum for the Dangerous and Criminally Insane was a series of ornate houses and buildings collectively appearing almost as a small city. As the carriage that held J. J., Sarah, and Martha entered the grounds, directly ahead of them was the Hospital and Admitting Building. To their right the drive led to a series of other buildings.

On the northeast corner of the institution sat Dr. Long's residence. His large, three-story home had four ornate columns along the front porch supporting an overhanging roof. A second-story balcony extended out to the columns directly over the front door. Three chimneys rose above the roof line of the beautiful home, one on each end, and one on the back. Leaded glass windows on either side of the large front door complimented a curved, leaded glass window that was set above. This curved window extended to the edges of both side windows.

To the west of the superintendent's residence were three beautiful buildings, all inter-connected. They were identified only with a number, one through three. Here, the male residents were housed. Buildings four, five and six, also inter-connected were to the west of, and slightly behind, the first set. Building five was restricted to women. It would be Martha Haney's new residence.

Building 5, Michigan Home for the Dangerous and Criminally Insane, Courtesy Archives of Michigan

All of the windows were barred.

Dr. Long's residence, the men's buildings and the women's building were all visible from South River Road. The rest of the asylum complex was located behind those and included a greenhouse, laundry, water tower, warehouse, garage, maintenance building, and slaughterhouse. There was also a coal yard and water reservoir. As part of their treatment, the inmates kept gardens, landscaped, and worked outside. On the east side of the grounds was a cemetery. Eight small houses served as residences for employees.

The dormitories - both mens' and womens' - were laid out the same. A long corridor lined with wooden benches separated each side. On the left side of the hall were four strong rooms used for problem inmates. Each strong room consisted of only a bed. On the right side of the corridor was a bathroom with three toilets and two sinks. Beyond the bathroom was a clothes room with individual areas for inmate clothing. The dormitory bedroom lay beyond the clothes room, which had six beds. There were three additional strong rooms at the end of each corridor.

Some of the other dorm buildings had large rooms where the inmates could sit. The large rooms were lined with rocking chairs.

J. J. and Sarah got out of the carriage and helped Martha down. The attendant led them inside the hospital and admitting building. Everything looked sterile. All of the walls were white and there seemed to be a chill inside. J. J. didn't know if he might be imagining the coolness simply because of where they were. He removed the shackles from Martha as she stood mumbling.

The nursing staff was there to take custody of Martha. They wore the customary white nurse's caps, white-collared tops and white sleeve cuffs. Their white aprons extended to the floor.

There was some paperwork for J. J. to sign attesting to the fact that Martha had been delivered to the asylum. The sheriff read the documents and signed his name. When he looked up, he was surprised to see Martha already being led down a long hallway and into an examination room.

That would be the last time J. J. Rehle ever saw Martha Haney.

The following day, J. J. spoke briefly with a reporter regarding Martha's journey to the asylum. When asked if there were any problems along the way, J. J. simply replied, "She had one or two spells."[70]

THE FINAL YEARS

It had been two-and-a-half years since Judge Rollin Person had ordered Martha Haney to be confined to the Michigan Home for the Dangerous and Criminally Insane. The sheer viciousness of the murder she committed stayed with him to the end of his days as a circuit court judge and beyond.

It was December 30, 1899, when 30 fellow lawyers from the Ingham County Bar Association entered Judge Person's courtroom and decorated the bench with carnations and roses before his arrival. Then they presented the soon-to-be former circuit judge with a handsome leather chair. The following day, 49-year-old Rollin Person re-entered private practice as one of Ingham County's most prominent lawyers.

There was no doubt but that he had made a name for himself over the previous nine years as a judge of the 30th Judicial Circuit.

Of note, in November, 1899, when Person, along with two other prominent Lansing legal experts, Arthur Tuttle and Judge Howard Weist, called for a grand jury to investigate irregularites in Govenor Hazen Pringree's handling of state affairs, they alleged the misuse of state funds and a criminal enterprise to sell military supplies to a fake company in Illinois. They believed that $50,000.00 in supplies had been sold to the Illinois company for $10,500. Those supplies were then sold back to the state for $62,000.00. While Judge Person left the bench prior to the end of the investigation, the charges brought resulted in several indictments, trials, and resignations.

After leaving the bench, Person joined the law firm of Charles F. Hammond, the same attorney he had appointed to represent Martha Haney. They shared the firm with attorney Harry Silsbee.

In 1912, Person was following a murder case being highlighted in the local newspaper with particular interest. Mary Lucas had been charged in the poisoning death of her neighbor, Pauline Fingle. What caught Person's attention was the accused's name. Lucas had been considered at one time to be Ingham County's first female lawyer, but

Person knew otherwise.

Mrs. Fingle, the murder victim, had attracted the attention of a man by the name of John Berenzc in what the local newspaper described as a "modern Lucretia Borgia" entanglement. Mary Lucas had already set her sights on Berenzc and was insanely jealous. When Mrs. Fingle disappeared, the Lansing Police Department began to investigate and discovered that the dirt in the Lucas basement had been recently disturbed. They also found shovels, and when they began to dig into the newly-turned dirt they discovered lime. Under questioning, Mary Lucas admitted to poisoning Mrs. Fingle with aconite, having put it into the victim's hot chocolate.

While Mary Lucas was on trial for the murder of her neighbor, the State Journal newspaper published an anonymous letter detailing the alleged murderer's questionable past. It was later learned that this anonymous letter had been written by former Circuit Court Judge Rollin Person.

In his letter to the newspaper, Person described having attended law school in Ann Arbor, and how he had stayed with a family by the name of Buckland. The Buckland's daughter was named Mary, and she was said to be the former Mary Lucas, having married a man by that last name. She told Person that John, her husband, had abandoned her to go out west. By her account, she and John Lucas were divorced and his name was not to be mentioned in the household.

After law school, Person left Ann Arbor and headed west, having occasion to room with a second lawyer near the Nebraska/Kansas border. While the two men were talking, they realized they shared one commonality: Ann Arbor, Michigan. The new roommate mentioned that his wife lived in Ann Arbor and she would be visiting him soon. Person immediately asked if his name was John Lucas, and after he responded affirmatively, Person detailed Lucas' wife's deceit. Person told him of how Mary had claimed she was divorced and told of her marriage to a man named Ayers, adding that they had a child together. John Lucas was furious. He showed Person a stack of letters written by his wife Mary. The letters even addressed John as her "dear husband." Person said that he and John Lucas never discussed the issue again.

Person's letter continued that after his stint as a young attorney in Nebraska, he returned to Michigan and began his practice in Lansing. One day while walking near the downtown, he noticed a sign that read: Lucas and Lucas, Attorneys. Curious, he went upstairs to the office. There he was greeted by his former acquaintance from Nebraska. Person never learned how or when John and his wife Mary reunited. And beyond being told that Mary's previous husband, Ayers, had died, he knew nothing more of the matter.

Mary Lucas primarily dealt in divorce matters, and after several of the cases she handled were "not made," her career as a barrister ended when she was summoned to a circuit judge's private office and confronted with the truth. The judge told her, "Mrs. Lucas, you know and I know that you are not an attorney and you will have to cease practicing here."[71]

After Mary was forced to quit practicing law in Ingham County, her husband John disappeared. Thereafter when Person would occasionally see her, she would tell him that John had been killed out west. Person saw very little of Mary after that. Then, one day when he read the headlines in the local papers, he felt compelled to spell out her deceitful past in an anonymous letter.

Mary Lucas was convicted of murdering her neighbor and sentenced to life in prison. On December 31, 1921 she was pardoned by Governor Sleeper, who cited her age as a consideration. She was 77 at the time.

In 1912, the same year that Mary Lucas was on trial for murdering her neighbor, Rollin Person became President of the Ingham County Bar Association.

Being a devout Presbyterian, Person liked to tell of how he had reduced the amount of liquor violation cases in the courts while he was a circuit judge. The typical fine for violators in the past had been $25. After several Fourth of July violations were brought before him, he cautioned each of the violators not to plead guilty unless they were, in fact, guilty. He would later say, "I fined them $200 each and you ought to have seen their faces."[72] The liquor violations ceased.

In 1912 and 1913, Person ran for the Michigan Supreme Court but was defeated. Person enjoyed 15 years in private practice after leaving the bench. Then, in 1915 he was appointed by the governor to fill the vacancy left by the death of Supreme Court Justice McHalvay. When Person completed the remaining two-year term as a Supreme Court Justice, he ran for re-election but was defeated just as he had been in 1912 and 1913. After the defeat in his re-election bid, he resumed private practice once again with the firm Person, Thomas, Shields and Silsbee in Lansing.

In the afternoon hours of June 2, 1917, just six months after leaving the bench as a Michigan Supreme Court Justice, Person left his office and returned to his home. Three hours later, he died unexpectedly.

Alva Cummins had served the citizens of Ingham County for two years as the prosecuting attorney. While serving as the prosecutor, he was partnered with L. B. McArthur in the firm of Cummins and McArthur. Upon his defeat in the 1898 election, he dedicated his efforts solely to private practice. In 1900 Cummins married his second wife, Fannie Fitch. His first wife had died shortly after childbirth, and Cummins had remained a widower for several years before he married Ms. Fitch.

After Cummins left the office of Ingham County's chief law enforcement officer, a decision he made while serving as the prosecutor was reviewed and addressed by the Michigan Supreme Court. The outcome likely affected law enforcement officers for years to come.

Submitted to the Court in 1899, the case centers on an allegation that as prosecutor, Cummins should have signed a certificate for witness fees in a particular matter.

The court record began:

> *Mandamus by Adoph Starmont to compel Alva M. Cummins, prosecuting attorney of Ingham County, to countersign a certificate for witness fees. From an order granting the writ, respondent brings certiorari. Reversed.*

The details of the case indicated a warrant had been issued for an offender by a Justice of the Peace. A clause in the warrant authorized the officer executing it to subpoena certain witnesses. Adolph Starmont was the one who ended up taking responsibility for the warrant. He also subsequently appeared and testified as a witness in the ensuing proceedings. For that he was awarded witness fees. Alva Cummins refused to countersign for the fees. He took the position that because Starmont was an officer attending court and receiving compensation for serving in that capacity, he wasn't entitled to further compensation as a witness. A writ of mandamus was issued by the lower court directing Cummins to sign for the witness fees.

After hearing arguments, the Michigan Supreme Court observed that Starmont was an officer in charge of a prisoner at the time of his testimony and was receiving compensation for that function when he testified. The court noted that the statute regarding witness fees was established to compensate a witness for his loss of time and wage incurred in having to appear in court. Starmont was not subpoenaed as a witness in the case, had not come to court as a witness, and had lost no time in fulfilling that role. The question became whether, given those facts, Starmont was entitled to additional compensation as a party and witness. The Court did not believe that he was. It held in favor of the respondent, former Prosecuting Attorney Alva Cummins.

Cummins became a member of the Michigan Democratic State

Central Committee in 1907. In 1911, he unsuccessfully ran for the 30th Circuit Court judgeship, a position once held by Rollin Person.

Cummins was certainly no stranger to the political arena. In both 1910 and 1912 he mounted campaigns in the Sixth District Congressional race. He was soundly defeated by over 5,000 votes in his first effort. The result was the same the second time around, but perhaps he took some comfort in that his margin of defeat was only 3,000 votes.

In 1917, like Rollin Person five years before him, Cummins served as President of the Ingham County Bar Association.

Cummins entered the race for Michigan's governor in 1922 and became a delegate to the Democratic National Convention in 1924. His last political race was in 1934 when he ran for a United States Senatorial seat.

At various points in his distinguished career, Cummins also served as President of the Lansing School Board of Education, as a member of the Public Utilities Commission, and as a member of Michigan's Liquor Control Commission.

In his final years, Cummins moved to Florida to enjoy his retirement. He eventually moved back to Michigan for the last two years of his life. On August 8, 1946, after attending a conference at the Lansing firm of Foster, Cummins, Snyder, Cameron and Foster, he traveled to his son's home in Okemos, where he suffered a fatal heart attack. Alva Cummins was 77 years old.

Charles Hammond continued in his private practice long after Martha's conviction for the murder of Mariah Haney. As her court-appointed attorney, Hammond's role was to make sure the rules were followed such that she was afforded a fair hearing. In reality, everything was, for the most part, a formality. Hammond, like Judge Person, Alva Cummins, J. J. Rehle, and everyone else involved, knew that Martha was destined for the asylum.

In addition to having served as the Ingham County Prosecuting Attorney, Hammond also had a colorful political career. He served as the Lansing city attorney, a member of the Lansing School Board (like Cummins), and as the Ingham County representative in the Michigan House three years before the Williamston murder. Long after Martha's sentencing, he also served as the Ingham County Bar Association president.

The early 1930s featured great advancements for the City of Lansing. Among them was the construction of a new landmark in the downtown area. The American State Bank building, towering over the rest of Lansing's skyline, opened across from the Capitol building. Charles F. Hammond, along with his son, Eugene, was among the first of the building's new occupants to move in. Three years after the law firm of Hammond and Hammond established that residency, Henry Schram joined their partnership.

Over time the firm's name changed to Hammond and Schram, and while Charles was largely retired, he appeared at the office door each morning wanting to help in some way.

On November 10, 1937, Charles Freemont Hammond, Martha Haney's court-appointed defense lawyer, passed away. While some may have argued otherwise, shortly after his death his son Eugene Hammond claimed that C. F. Hammond was responsible for establishing the oldest law firm in all of Ingham County. .

Long after the arrival of Williamston's notorious killer at his asylum, Dr. Oscar R. Long remained the institution's Superintendent. In an effort to advance the asylum's success, he continued his use of the homeopathic approach to treat its inmates. Unless an inmate was violent toward a fellow inmate, he or she was allowed to roam free within the building of their residence.

It was a year after Martha Haney's institutionalization when Dr. Long was awarded an honorary degree from the Homeopathic Medical School at the University of Michigan. In 1900, he was offered a position as dean of that same medical school. He declined the position. Nevertheless, during the 1890s and into the early part of the 1900s, Dr. Long served as a lecturer at the University of Michigan. His topics dealt with mental and nervous diseases. He also became an expert witness in matters involving medical-legal interrelationships work.

Dr. Long was a well-respected member of the medical community. As superintendent at the asylum, he was considered an excellent administrator because the asylum ran so smoothly. In addition, he was a very strict disciplinarian and well known for his economical and efficient approach to administration.

The beauty of the asylum grounds was largely attributable to him, not only because of the location, which he personally chose, but because of the artistic arrangement of the buildings, which he personally supervised. He was known to have excellent taste.

During the course of his service at the asylum in Ionia, Dr. Oscar Long became recognized as a leading man in the field of his expertise throughout the entire state of Michigan and beyond. He was also greatly valued as a citizen in Ionia.

Dr. Long died suddenly on September 10, 1914 at the age of 64.

Alfy Haney, although distraught over the death of his aged mother, enjoyed his newfound fame immediately following her sudden and gruesome demise. He never spoke of Martha again.

Three years after his mother's death, Alfy became acquainted with a woman named Alice Cornell who lived in Lansing. Their relationship immediately grew into something more than a simple friendship, and Alfy moved in with her. It didn't take long for the neighbors to notice, and word spread that the two unmarried lovers were living together. They were promptly arrested. Then Prosecuting Attorney Arthur J. Tuttle charged both Alfy and Alice with lewd and lascivious cohabitation. On August 13, 1900, Alfred Haney pled guilty to the charge. On September 10, he was sentenced to ten months in the Detroit House of Corrections for his lack of judgment and decency.

Alfy's girlfriend Alice, also facing incarceration for her indiscretions, pled guilty to the charge. On September 22nd, her sentence of eight months in the Detroit House of Corrections was deferred, and she was released on her own recognizance.

Throughout his remaining years, Alfy continued the only life he'd ever known as a laborer on the streets. After their arrest, and Alfy's subsequent incarceration, Alfy and Alice were married and together they lived in Lansing.

Alice Haney died by 1910, leaving Alfy a widower. He had moved back to Williamstown Township with his brother Riley, who lived north of the village near Sherwood Road. Riley had a wife and two daughters living at the same residence. For years, the two men could be seen wandering around the village, hunched over with their hands clasped behind their backs as they traversed the streets. Riley passed away in 1923.

With no money and no means of support, coupled with his age, in 1930 Alfy found himself living in the county's poorhouse on Dobie Road in Okemos. He lived there until he was 76 years old when he suffered a stroke. Alf passed away on August 23, 1937. Every day of his life, up to the day of his death, he was haunted by the horrible memory of that April day in 1897.

After Martha's delivery to the asylum in Ionia, life almost returned to normal for J. J. at the Ingham County Jail. While the daily routine was much as it had been, J. J. found it difficult to put the murder of Mariah Haney out of his mind. He often thought about his own three daughters and how close in age they were to Martha. When he thought of Martha's three children, Ernest, George, and Emily, he couldn't help but think of his own grandchildren and couldn't quite understand how any mother could simply give away her children. His daughter Anna, whom he saw the most because she was married to his undersheriff Martin, had already given J. J. and Sarah a granddaughter named Muriel, and they were expecting another child within the next five weeks. The thoughts of the murder and Martha's entire miserable life haunted J. J. daily. Yet his routine demanded his attention.

In early May, within two weeks after the Williamston murder, J. J. had three prisoners from the jail come outside to help carry in some wood. With his mind wandering and thinking of recent events, the sheriff let his guard down. The three prisoners snuck away. Upon realizing they were gone, J. J. gave chase and quickly captured them a mile away. It was never considered a successful escape because J. J. had recaptured the criminals so quickly and returned them to the lockup without further incident.

After the infamous murder in Williamston, like her husband, Sarah tried to settle back into a quiet day-to-day life at the jail. There was nothing quiet about a day later that September however. Preventing a jail escape while J. J. was away on business, Sarah made headlines in Detroit's Evening News, The National Police Gazette, and the New York Times when she caught prisoner Al Stone trying to break out.

Known as "Stoney," Al Stone had escaped from the Ingham County Jail in June of 1895 after being arrested for robbery. In his previous escape, he had made a hole in the jail floor and escaped with a prisoner named Cummins. After his capture, he served 15 months of hard labor at a Toledo workhouse. Being somewhat defeated when he was arrested again after returning to Mason, and before he could be searched at the jail, his plan was to take a bottle from his pocket and swallow the contents. The turnkey couldn't stop Stone, and he thought the inmate might have ingested poison. Despite this fear, by the next morning Stoney had fully recovered. Since his first attempt at escape by feigning a suicide attempt had failed, he decided to take a different approach.

While feeding the prisoners soon after "Stoney's" last escape attempt, the turnkey noticed the prisoner was missing from his cell. He and another deputy began an immediate search of the jail and found him hiding in the washroom armed with two knives. After a brief scuffle between the convict and the lawmen, "Stoney" was able to escape from his would be captors. He ran for the section of the jail where a lever hung to open all of the jail cells at the same time. Hearing the commotion, Sarah grabbed a gun and confronted "Stoney" just before he as able to raise more havoc. Stone immediately surrendered.

The Evening News in Detroit offered this rendition of the attempted jail break that was thwarted by the sheriff's wife:

> "Mrs. John Rehle, wife of the sheriff of Ingham County, prevented a jail delivery by holding the prisoners at bay with a cocked revolver. She caught Al Stone cutting a hole through the wall and pointing a revolver exclaimed: "You attempt to use that knife, and I will shoot you." The prisoner begged. "I did not shoot," said Mrs. Rehle last night, "but I felt just like it. I could have winged him, I know, and then he would not give any more trouble." "You would have probably shot at his feet." "No, I would have started to cut off his toes, just above the neck. Yes, I am used to firearms. Have lived on the farm all my life, and when my husband would return from a hunting trip, I would tell him I could beat him shooting at a mark, and I did, many a time, too, both with a rifle and revolver. No I am not afraid of any of the prisoners, and, in the absence of my husband, or turnkey, I wait on and fed [sic] them myself."

Mrs. Rehle is 49 years old, the mother of four children, and a refined Christian woman, who does much for deserving prisoners."[73]

Courtesy of Steve Westlake and the National Police Gazette Enterprises, LLC.

It was in early October, shortly after Stoney's escape attempt, when the headlines in the local papers read *Shooting Affray in Wheatfield*. In some ways, the investigation of this offense paralleled the case of Martha Haney.

J. J. had been notified by Deputy Loranger of the shooting. Simeon Kent, who lived on a farm adjoining that of his brother Seth, had gotten into an argument with him on the way back from Mason on a beautiful fall afternoon. The brothers had once been very close, but after Simeon lost his wife, he adopted a lifestyle that his brother didn't approve, and it was suspected that they fought over that topic. After returning to one of the farms, Simeon immediately went into the house and grabbed a double-barreled shotgun. He returned to the yard and fired both barrels. The first shot struck Seth in the eye, while the second blast hit him in his side. Simeon quickly fled.

Williamston's Dr. Coad was quickly notified of the shooting, and he, in turn, contacted Deputy Loranger. Both men headed to the farm, and, while Seth was being treated by Dr. Coad, Loranger was able to locate his brother nearby and place him under arrest. Simeon was taken back to the calaboose in Williamston. Once Simeon was secured in the jail, J. J. was notified. As part of his investigation, J. J. spoke with Seth, who absolutely refused to swear out a complaint against his brother.

J. J. wasn't quite sure what to do. He knew Simeon should be charged, but what was the best course of action if Seth wasn't going to cooperate? J. J. called Alva Cummins. Cummins ordered J. J. to swear out two complaints against Simeon. The first complaint would be for assault with intent to kill, and the second was assault with intent to do great bodily harm less than murder. Cummins told J. J. that Simeon Ken would be charged with one offense or the other.

After Simeon was taken back to the Ingham County Jail, he ranted and raved all night in his cell. The following day he could recall nothing of the attempt on his brother's life. In early January of 1898, his trial before a jury resulted in a verdict of not guilty of the complaint, but insane at the time of the shooting. In addition, the jury found Kent to still be suffering from insanity. With that, Judge Rollin Person ordered that Simeon Kent be confined to the Michigan Asylum for the Dangerous and Criminally Insane.

Like he had done less than a year earlier in Martha Haney's case, J. J. loaded Kent onto the train for the long ride to Ionia and delivered him without incident.

The November 1898 elections were fast approaching. Michigan law allowed for only a two-year term for the sheriff, so J. J. was obliged to run again. While the Haney homicide and the Kent shooting, both in Wheatfield Township, had been taxing on him, J. J. still enjoyed his work.

In October, the Democratic People's and Union Silver conventions convened.[74] With acclamation, every county official was re-nominated for their positions amid much affair. The Ingham County Democrat newspaper read, "Such harmonious action nearly threw the republican enemy into convulsions." The mere mention of former Presidential candidate William Jennings Bryan threw the crowd into thunderous applause and cheers. Even republicans were paying homage to some of their democratic contenders by conceding that the county officers had performed their duties honestly and faithfully. The Ingham County Democrat, in its coverage of the convention, said:

> "With the good work performed by the convention, the harmony and good feeling that prevailed there is no doubt that the successful ticket was selected on this day."

Republican supervisor Urquhart of Lansing singled J. J. out for praise by saying that the bills he had presented had been the fairest ever.[75]

At the local convention, Frank L. Dodge was honored to give the nod to J. J. as the democratic nominee for the office of the sheriff.

The Ingham County Democrat made one more push for J. J. just prior to the election:

> "During Sheriff Rehle's term there has not been an escape from the jail. This record will add to his majority."

Despite the accolades and much to his continuant's surprise, J. J. was defeated in the 1898 election by the republican candidate, William H. Porter.

THE FINAL YEARS | 143

Following the election, J. J. and Sarah moved back to their Burkley Road farm in Wheatfield Township southwest of Williamston. Sarah's health slowly began to deteriorate, so after two years they moved back to Mason to a home on Okemos Street.

The couple celebrated their 40th wedding anniversary in 1909.

Sarah had become a member of the Eastern Star, a Freemasonry organization with teachings based upon the bible. The female members of the organization had to be a relative of a Freemason, and J. J. was. Sarah attended an Eastern Star meeting in Mason on Janaury 2 and was in normal health. The following day while visiting a neighbor, she developed severe stomach pains. Her sudden decline in health continued over the next ten days. On January 12, 1912, the wife of the former Ingham County Sheriff passed away.

J. J. continued living quietly in the Mason area for eleven more years. On May 18, 1923, he went to visit his daughter Elizabeth and her husband John Fink on St. Joe Road near Lansing. While there, J. J. became suddenly ill and suffered a stroke. He died that afternoon at the Fink home.

On May 21, J. J.'s funeral was held at the home where he died. It was said that during his lifetime, J. J.'s straightforwardness, honesty, and integrity had been prized in the farming community. He was buried next to his loving wife, Sarah, in Mason's Maple Grove Cemetery.

Martha Haney lived out her days at the Michigan Home for the Dangerous and Criminally Insane as best she could. When not consumed by one of her fits, she was allowed to roam free within the building where she was housed but she was confined to the floor on which her room was located. The doors were always locked, and the bars were secured to the windows to prevent any attempts at escape.

On the day that J. J. delivered her to her new residence, she was subjected to a medical examination, as all new patients were. As a result, it was discovered that Martha suffered from consumption. The constant cough she had developed became worse, and her lack of appetite and weight loss were symptoms of a much a larger problem. Often times Martha would refuse to eat, much like she had during her brief incarceration at the Ingham County Jail following the murder of Mariah Haney.

Tuberculosis had peaked during the eighteenth and nineteenth century. The effects of the illness included a drying or consuming cough, and the disease was often fatal among middle- aged adults. It had become known as the great white plague. Perfect breeding grounds for the disease became commonplace due to population density and poor sanitary conditions around the country. The disease was often referred to as a romantic disease because of its slow progression, meaning that it allowed for a "good death," or one that allowed sufferers time to arrange their affairs prior to succumbing.

Consumption, or Phthisis as it was also called, was so prevalent during Martha's lifetime, a German doctor said of the disease:

> "If the importance of a disease for mankind is measured from the number of fatalities which are due to it, then tuberculosis must be considered much more important than those most feared infectious diseases, plague, cholera, and the like. Statistics have shown that half of all humans die from tuberculosis."[76]

The scientific advancement that led to understanding the disease and its contagious nature also led to the need for institutions to house people suffering from it. Some of the surgical procedures used in an attempt to intervene included collapsing a person's lung in an effort to allow the lesions upon the lung to heal.

Whatever medical interventions may have been tried, if any, in Martha's case didn't work.

Seventeen months after severing her mother-in-law's head in a fit of insane rage and displaying it on a plate as a gift to her husband, then setting the corpse ablaze, Martha Haney died at the Asylum for the Dangerous and Criminally Insane in Ionia.

Martha Haney's death certificate, Courtesy "Seeking Michigan"

Notes

The house where Mariah Haney's life came to an abrupt and violent end stood until the mid-1990s. It had been lived in for many years following that horrible day in 1897. It was eventually donated to the Northeast Ingham Emergency Services Authority for training and was burned so firefighters could sharpen their skills. The foundation still lies buried where the home once stood.

The train depot in Williamston still exists, though in 1979, fear of it being demolished caused the entire community to rally, and it was moved to its present location on West Grand River. It now houses the Williamston Depot Museum.

The Michigan Asylum for the Dangerous and Criminally Insane is no longer in existence. In 1911, the name of the facility was changed to the Ionia State Hospital, and it operated for many years after that. Today, none of the original buildings exist, and the Michigan Reformatory, Michigan's second oldest penal institution, which was originally built at the same time as the asylum, has expanded and occupies the location where the asylum once stood.

While doing research for this book, the author frequently turned to *Ancestry.com* in his efforts to locate information. In attempting to find any living relatives of Alfred and Martha Haney, the author found the name of a person he believes was their daughter Emily. Unfortunately she died in 1960. Emily did have children, but beyond that, the author was unable to locate any additional information.

The information regarding the daughter of Alfred and Martha Haney was confirmed through records located at the Archives of Michigan, as were the names of the other two children mentioned in this book.

It is likely Martha Haney would have been diagnosed today as being schizophrenic. Those who suffer from such a disease show symptoms of altered perceptions of reality, significant loss of contact with reality, feelings of being constantly watched and believing others may be trying to harm them. Those afflicted may speak in strange and confusing ways. They have difficulties negotiating day-to-day life activities and experience trouble in distinguishing between real and imagined worlds.

The majority of schizophrenic cases appear in the late teens or early adulthood. Many of those who suffer from schizophrenia today can be treated over the long-term period and can enjoy life while functioning within their family and the community.

Schizophrenia has a strong hereditary component, but heredity only influences genetics. A person's life is not determined by it.

All of the information provided in the news accounts of Martha Haney's crime, her life before the murder, and her actions in the jail suggest that she suffered from schizophrenia. Beyond that, her mother died in Ionia, and while there hasn't been a direct link to the asylum, that is certainly a possibility. In addition, the author's research indicates that Martha's daughter, and possibly her granddaughter, may have died in an institution.

Martha's exact diagnosis from the doctors at the asylum is something the author was not able to determine. Mental health records within the State of Michigan are sealed and not accessible to the public at large.

More out of curiosity than anything else, the author attempted to locate the burial places of several people involved in this case. With much difficulty, the author was finally able to locate the cemetery where Alfred Haney is buried. Martha Haney's burial location remains a mystery, as does the location of Mariah Haney's grave.

Bibliography

Bench and Bar of Michigan: A Volume of History and Biography, 1897, Chicago The Century Publishing and Engraving Company

History of Ingham and Eaton Counties, Michigan, Part II, History of Ingham County, 1880, D. W. Ensign and Co.

Let the Record Show: A Legal History of Ingham County Michigan, 1997, Michigan State University Press

History of Williamston, 1838-1963: A Story of Real People and One Hundred Twenty Five Years of a Country Town, 1963, B. M. Merrifield and L. G. Howarth

A Brief History of Williamston, Michigan, 2008, Kenneth V. Zichi

History of Ionia County: Her People, Industries, and Institutions, 2012, Forgotten Books

The University of Michigan, an Encyclopedic Survey, Part 1, History Administration, 1942, University of Michigan Press

Historical Michigan, Ingham County, 1924, National Historical Association

University Homeopathic Observer, Volume 1, http://books.google.rw/books/about/University_Homoeopathic_Observer.html?id=7kniAAAAMAAJ

The Compiled Laws of the State of Michigan, 1897, Volume III, 2012, Rare Books Club

Michigan State Gazetteer and Business Directory of 1897, Volume XIII

A History of Mental Health Nursing, 1993, http://books.google.com/books?id=vo46Jqvu_8oC&printsec=frontcover&dq=a+history+of+mental+health+nursing&hl=en&sa=X&ei=koB6VPyFA4nasATK5IGIDw&ved=0CDIQ6AEw AA#v=onepage&q=a%20history%20of%20mental%20health%20nursing&f=falseNelson Thornes, Ltd.

New England Medical Gazette, 1866, University of Michigan Library, http://books.google.com/books?id=wt9XAAAAMAAJ&pg=PA96&dq=new+england+medical+gazette+1866&hl=en&sa=X&ei=d4F6VND9G9CwsAS0uoK4AQ&ved=0CB0Q6AEwAA#v=onepage&q=new%20england%20medical%20gazette%201866&f=false

Michigan Genealogy: Sources and Resources, 1897 Genealogical Publishing Company

Lansing: City on the Grand, 1836-1939, 2003, MacLean, James and Whitford, Craig, Arcadia Publishing, Charleston, SC

Medical Century, Volume V, 1897, 2012 Ulan Press

The University Paladium, Volume 1, 1874, http://books.google.com/books/about/ The_University_Palladium.html?id=JwviAAAAMAAJ

Ten Days in a Mad-House, Nellie Bly, 2011, Create Space Independent Publishing Platform

Michigan Reports: Cases Decided in the Supreme Court of Michigan, Volume 120, p 629, Starmont v Cummins 1897 Sears Roebuck & Company Catalogue, 2007, Skyhorse, Publishing

Stories From Williamston's Past, 2014, Lutzke, Mitch, Schuler Books, Grand Rapids, MI

The Michiganensian,, 1897, University of Michigan

Lansing, Michigan City Directory, 1896

Lansing, Michigan City Directory, 1894

Ionia Sentinel, April 30, 1897, Horrible Deed of an Insane Woman at Williamston

Capital City Democrat, Lansing, Michigan, October 26, 1898

Ingham County Democrat, January 7, 1897, Board of Supervisors Approves County Officers Bonds

Ingham County Democrat, October 8, 1896

Ingham County Democrat, October 15, 1896, Union Nominee For Sheriff

Ingham County Democrat, October 29, 1896

Ingham County Democrat, January 14, 1897

Ingham County Democrat, January 21, 1897

Ingham County Democrat, January 28, 1897

Ingham County Democrat, January 30, 1897

Ingham County Democrat, March 4, 1897

Ingham County Democrat, March 18, 1897

Ingham County Democrat, April 15, 1897

Ingham County Democrat, April 22, 1897, Local and General News

Ingham County Democrat, April 29, 1897, Awful Deed

Ingham County Democrat, May 6, 1897, Mrs. Haney on Trial

Ingham County Democrat, August 18, 1909

Ingham County Democrat, October 6, 1898

Ingham County Democrat, October 20, 1898

Ingham County Democrat, November 3, 1898

Ingham County Democrat, November 10, 1898, County Turned Over

Marshall Statesman, April 30, 1897, Beheads Her Victim

The Evening News, Detroit, April 24, 1897, Insane Cunning

The Evening News, Detroit, Wednesday, September 22, 1897, A Woman Who Can Shoot

Detroit Free Press, April 24, 1897

Detroit Free Press, April 26, 1897

Detroit Free Press, August 17, 1897, The Ingham County Jail

The State Republican, January 14, 1897

The State Republican, January 18, 1897

The State Republican, January 19, 1897

Lansing Journal, April 28, 1897

Kalamazoo Daily Telegraph, April 24, 1897, Head on a Platter

Williamson Enterprise, July 23, 1890

Williamston Enterprise, April 28, 1897, Frightful

Ingham County News, April 29, 1897, Revolting Crime

Ingham County News, May 6, 1897, A Horrible Crime

Ingham County News, May 8, 1897

Ingham County News, October 1, 1936

Sunday News Tribune, April 25, 1897, In Jail at Mason

Sunday News Tribune, April 25, 1897, Butted Her Head

National Police Gazette, October 9, 1897, Brave Woman Foils Convicts

Fort Wayne News, April 21, 1897, Wife's Gift

New York Times, Sept 23, 1897, Plucky Woman

St. John's News, April 29, 1897, Devil Is Even in the Women

Adrian Evening Telegraph, April 24, 1897, p 2, Insane Woman Chops off Her Mother-in-Law's Head

The Grand Rapids Democrat, April 24, 1897, p 2, Horrible- Young Woman Beheads Her Mother-in-Law

1897 Williamston Murder, Cara Steinberg and Chelsea Robinson
http://www.helpguide.org/mental/schizophrenia_symptom.htm

Endnotes

1. History of Williamstown, http://ingham.migenweb.net/Williamstown.html

2. Williamston Depot Museum, http://www.williamstonmuseum.org/williamston-depot-history.html

3. http://www.williamstonmuseum.org/williamston-depot-history.html

4. History of Wheatfield Township http://ingham.migenweb.net/Wheatfield.html

5. Capital City Democrat, Lansing, Mich., October 26, 1898

6. http://ingham.migenweb.net/Wheatfield.html

7. The Election of 1896, http://www.authentichistory.com/1865-1897/4-1896election/index.html

8. Ingham County Democrat, October 8, 1896

9. Ingham County Democrat, Democrats, Populists and Union Silver Voters, October 29, 1896

10. Ingham County Democrat, January 14, 1897

11. The State Republican, January 18, 1897

12. The State Republican, January 19, 1897

13. The State Republican, January 14, 1897

14 Ingham County Democrat, March 4, 1897

15 Detroit Free Press, April 26, 1897

16 Detroit Free Press, April 26, 1897

17 Williamston Enterprise, April 28, 1897

18 Williamston Enterprise, April 28, 1897

19 Awful Deed, Detroit Free Press, April 24, 1897

20 Awful Deed, Ingham County Democrat, April 29, 1897

21 http://ingham.migenweb.net/Wheatfield.html

22 http://ingham.migenweb.net/Wheatfield.html

23 Williamston Enterprise, July 23, 1890

24 Awful Deed, Ingham County Democrat, April 29, 1897

25 Awful Deed, Ingham County Democrat, April 29, 1897

26 Insane Woman Chops Off Mother in Law's Head, Adrian Evening Telegraph, April 24, 1897

27 Frank Shumway, http://www.petershumway.org/nti/nti00614.htm

28 Frightful, Williamston Enterprise, April 28, 1897

29 Detroit Free Press, April 24, 1897

30 Detroit Free Press, April 24, 1897

31 Revolting Crime, Ingham County News, April 29, 1897

32 Martha E. Pierce, http://trees.ancestry.com/tree/28843857/person/12103644228

33 Awful Deed, Ingham County Democrat, April 29, 1897

34 Ingham County News, May 8, 1897

35 Application for Admission to Rocky Beach Benevolent Association, 1891

36 Frightful, Williamston Enterprise, April 28, 1897

37 Frightful, Williamston Enterprise, April 28, 1897

38 Frightful, Williamston Enterprise, April 28, 1897

39 http://ingham.migenweb.net/Williamstown.html

40 Frightful, Williamston Enterprise, April 28, 1897

41 Frightful, Williamston Enterprise, April 28, 1897

42 Frightful, Williamston Enterprise, April 28, 1897

43 Revolting Crime, Ingham County News, April 29, 1897

44 Awful Deed, Ingham County Democrat, April 29, 1897

45 The Compiled Laws of the State of Michigan, 1897, Volume III

46 The Compiled Laws of the State of Michigan, 1897, Volume III

47 The Compiled Laws of the State of Michigan, 1897, Volume III

48 In Jail at Mason, Sunday News Tribune, April 25, 1897

49 In Jail at Mason, Sunday News Tribune, April 25, 1897

50 Insane Cunning, Evening News Detroit, April 24, 1897

51 Insane Cunning, Evening News Detroit, April 24, 1897

52 Insane Cunning, Evening News Detroit, April 24, 1897

53 Butted Her Head, Sunday News Tribune, April 24, 1897

54 In Jail at Mason, Sunday News Tribune, April 25, 1897

55 People v Martha Haney, Ingham County Criminal Complaint, April 24, 1897

56 People v Martha Haney, Ingham County Warrant, April 24, 1897

57 In Jail at Mason, Sunday News Tribune, April 25, 1897

58 Ingham County Democrat, April 29, 1897

59 People v Martha Haney, Warrant Return, April 26, 1897

60 People v Martha Haney, Ingham County Circuit Court file, April 27, 1897

61 Ingham County Democrat, May 6, 1897

62 United Kingdom House of Lords Decisions, 8 ER 718, [1843] UKHL J16

63 People v Martha Haney, Commission Letter to the Circuit Court, April 28, 1897

64 The Compiled Laws of the State of Michigan, 1897, Volume III

65 Peter Nolan, A History of Mental Health Nursing, 1993, Stanley Thornes, Ltd.

66 Peter Nolan, A History of Mental Health Nursing, 1993, Stanley Thornes, Ltd.

67 Peter Nolan, A History of Mental Health Nursing, 1993, Stanley Thornes, Ltd.

68 Ten Days in a Mad-House, Nellie Bly, p 66

69 Bly, p 66

70 Mrs. Haney in Court, Ingham County Democrat, April 29, 1897

71 Richard Frazier, David Thomas, Let the Record Show, East Lansing: Michigan State University Press, 1997, 156

72 Frazier, and Thomas, 13

73 The Evening News, Detroit, Wednesday, September 22, 1897, A Woman Who Can Shoot

74 A Love Feast, Ingham County Democrat, Oct. 6, 1898

75 Rehle Endorsed, Ingham County Democrat, October 20, 1898

76 Die Atiologne Der Tuberculose, Robert Roch, 1882

CPSIA information can be obtained
at www.ICGtesting.com
Printed in the USA
FSOW02n1645280917
39250FS